Coordinating physical education across the primary school

THE SUBJECT LEADER'S HANDBOOKS

Series Editor: Mike Harrison, Centre for Primary Education,
School of Education, The University of Manchester,
Oxford Road, Manchester, M13 9DP

Coordinating mathematics across the primary school
Tony Brown

Coordinating English at Key Stage 1
Mick Waters and Tony Martin

Coordinating English at Key Stage 2
Mick Waters and Tony Martin

Coordinating science across the primary school
Lynn D. Newton and Douglas P. Newton

Coordinating information and communications technology across the
primary school
Mike Harrison

Coordinating art across the primary school
Judith Piotrowski, Robert Clements and Ivy Roberts

Coordinating design and technology across the primary school
Alan Cross

Coordinating geography across the primary school
John Halocha

Coordinating history across the primary school
Julie Davies and Jason Redmond

Coordinating music across the primary school
Sarah Hennessy

Coordinating religious education across the primary school
Derek Bastide

Coordinating physical education across the primary school
Carole Raymond

Management skills for SEN coordinators
Sylvia Phillips, Jennifer Goodwin and Rosita Heron

Building a whole school assessment policy
Mike Wintle and Mike Harrison

The curriculum coordinator and the OFSTED inspection
Phil Gadsby and Mike Harrison

Coordinating the curriculum in the smaller primary school
Mick Waters

Coordinating physical education across the primary school

Carole Raymond

FALMER PRESS

Taylor & Francis Group

UK	The Falmer Press, 1 Gunpowder Square, London, EC4A 3DE
USA	The Falmer Press, Taylor & Francis Inc., 1900 Frost Road, Suite 101, Bristol, PA 19007

First published in 1998

A catalogue record for this book is available from the British Library

Library of Congress Cataloging-in-Publication Data are available on request

ISBN 0 7507 0693 7 paper

Jacket design by Carla Turchini

Typeset in 10/14pt Melior and printed by Graphicraft Typesetters Ltd., Hong Kong.

Contents

Part one
The role of the PE coordinator

Part two
What the PE coordinator needs to know

Part three
Whole school policies and schemes of work

Part four
Monitoring for Quality

Part five
Resources for teaching and learning

List of figures

Acknowledgments

During the preparation of this book I consulted many people and numerous publications. The material presented draws together my findings about what I and other experienced colleagues regard as 'good practice', it reflects my visits to schools, interviews and meetings with teachers and coordinators, dialogue with colleagues in higher education and the advisory service, and a review of recent and relevant literature, including exemplar materials and research findings. I am grateful to all of these friends and colleagues for the help, encouragement and guidance they offered so willingly.

A few individual thank-yous are particularly appropriate: To Kath Keeley, Claire Hamer, Jodie Harris, Bob Foale, Libby Mailey and Linda Rolfe for participating in my preparatory collection of data. Their knowledge and thoughtful suggestions showed sensitivity and was much appreciated. To Carole Parnell and Tony Cooper, whose reviews provided valuable comments that strengthened the manuscript.

I am grateful to the following for permission to reproduce copyright material:
English Sports Council, Physical Education Association of the United Kingdom, Stanley Thornes Publishers, British Association of Advisers and Lecturers in PE, Devon County Council, Hereford and Worcester County Council and the North Eastern Education and Library Board of Northern Ireland.

While every effort has been made to acknowledge all my sources of information, particularly those bound by copyright, in a few cases this has proved impossible and I take this opportunity to offer my apologies to any copyright holders whose right I may have unwittingly infringed.

To Julie Williams, gratitude for her assistance in finalising the manuscript.

Dedication

Thank you to my mother and late father for their love, support and encouragement. To Kate, Rebecca, Abigail, Gareth and Alexander whose youth and vitality give added impetus to my pursuit of quality physical education for all young people.

List of acronyms

BAALPE	British Association of Advisers and Lecturers in Physical Education
CCW	Curriculum Council for Wales
CEP	Career Entry Profile
DES	Department of Education
DfEE	Department for Education and Employment
ECP	Extra Curriculum Provision
EKSD	End of Key Stage Description
HMI	Her Majesty's Inspectorate
NEELB	North Eastern Education and Library Board
NCC	National Curriculum Council
NQT	Newly Qualified Teacher
OFSTED	Office for Standards in Education
PE	Physical Education
PEAUK	Physical Education of the United Kingdom
PGCE	Postgraduate Certificate in Education
PoS	Programme of Study
SCAA	School Curriculum and Assessment Authority
SCITT	School Based Initial Teacher Training
SEAC	Schools Examination and Assessment Council
TTA	Teacher Training Agency

Series editor's preface

This book has been prepared for primary teachers charged with the responsibility of acting as the coordinators for physical education (PE) within their schools. It forms part of a series of new publications that set out to advise such teachers on the complex issues of improving teaching and learning through managing each element of the primary school curriculum.

Why is there a need for such a series? Most authorities recognise, after all, that the quality of primary children's work and learning depends upon the skills of their class teacher, not in the structure of management systems, policy documents or the titles and job descriptions of staff.

Many today recognise that school improvement equates directly to the improvement of teaching so surely all tasks, other than imparting subject knowledge, are merely a distraction for the committed primary teacher.

Nothing should take teachers away from their most important role, that is, serving the best interests of the class of children in their care and this book and the others in the series does not wish to diminish that mission. However, the increasing complexity of the primary curriculum and society's expanding expectations, makes it very difficult for the class teacher to keep up to date with every development. Within traditional subject areas there has been an explosion of knowledge and new fields introduced such as science, technology, design, problem solving and health education, not to mention the uses of computers. These are now considered entitlements for primary children. Furthermore, we now expect all children to succeed at these studies, not just the fortunate few. All this has overwhelmed a class teacher system largely unchanged since the inception of primary schools.

Primary class teachers cannot possibly be an expert in every aspect of the curriculum they are required to teach. To whom can they turn for help? It is unrealistic to assume that such support will be available from the headteacher whose responsibilities have grown ever wider since the 1988 Educational Reform Act. Constraints, including additional staff costs, and the loss of benefits from the strength and security of the class teacher system, militate against wholesale adoption of specialist or semi-specialist teaching. Help therefore has to come from exploiting the talents of teachers themselves, in a process of mutual support. Hence primary schools have chosen many and varied systems of consultancy or subject coordination which best suit the needs of their children and the current expertise of the staff.

In fact, curriculum leadership functions in primary schools have increasingly been shared with class teachers through the policy of curriculum coordination for the past twenty years, especially to improve the consistency of work in language and mathematics. Since then each school has developed their own system and the series recognises that the system each reader is part of will be a compromise between the ideal and the possible. Campbell and Neill (1994) show that by 1991 nearly nine out of every ten primary class teachers had such responsibility and the average number of subjects each was between 1.5 and 2.2 (depending on the size of school).

These are the people for whom this series sets out to help to do this part of their work. The books each deal with specific issues whilst at the same time providing an overview of general themes in the management of the subject curriculum. The term *subject leader* is used in an inclusive sense and combines the two major roles that such teachers play when they have responsibility for subjects and aspects of the primary curriculum.

The books each deal with:
■ *coordination* — a role which emphasises harmonising, bringing together, making links, establishing routines and common practice; and
■ *subject leadership* — a role which emphasises providing information, offering expertise and direction, guiding the development of the subject, and raising standards.

The purpose of the series is to give practical guidance and support to teachers; in particular what to do and how to do it. They each offer help on the production, development and review of policies and schemes of work; the organisation of resources; and developing strategies for improving the management of the subject curriculum.

Each book in the series contains material that subject managers will welcome and find useful in developing their subject expertise and in tackling problems of enthusing and motivating staff.

Each book has five parts.
1 The review and development of the different roles coordinators are asked to play.
2 Updating subject knowledge and subject pedagogical knowledge.
3 Developing and maintaining policies and schemes of work.
4 Monitoring work within the school to enhance the continuity of teaching and progression in pupil's learning.
5 Resources and contacts.

Although written primarily for teachers who are PE coordinators, Carole Raymond's book offers practical guidance and ideas for anyone in the school who has a responsibility for the physical education, curriculum including teachers with an overall role in coordinating the whole or key stage curriculum and the deputy head and the headteacher.

In making the book easily readable Carole has drawn upon her considerable experience as a leader and lecturer in physical education, and on the experiences of others including primary coordinators, teachers, advisers, *OFSTED* inspectors and teacher educators. The short training tasks and case study material included will be particularly useful to those who are new to the job or have recently changed schools.

Mike Harrison, Series Editor
January 1998

Introduction

This book is one of a series focusing on the role of the subject coordinator in primary schools. At the outset, authors with varied teaching experience met to consider the subject coordinator's role and prepare an analytical framework focusing on key areas of responsibility which would form the basis for the text. One of the biggest discussions concerned 'Are you managers, leaders or coordinators?' It would appear from advertisements that schools have 'coordinators', these are part of 'management' teams, but recent government initiatives promote 'leaders'. The words are inevitably interrelated and quite often used synonymously. This book is therefore an introduction to management and leadership for Physical Education (PE) coordinators.

The role of coordinators as 'middle managers' has increased over recent years, more recently this has focused on subjects. This is partly because of the diverse curriculum in schools, ongoing government initiatives and an increase in accountability. In fact we have now reached a situation when there are few members of staff in primary schools who do not have some form of coordinating responsibility; there are also new qualifications for subject leaders. This book is for all those staff with responsibility for coordinating PE.

I have tried to make the book 'user friendly' by avoiding jargon and by offering practical guidance and ideas related to the coordinator's role and responsibilities. The material is drawn from recognised 'good' practice and makes use of coordinators' experiences, as well as management theory. There is a research base to the book with data collated from interviews and an analysis of documentation (school handbooks, OFSTED, literature). This has involved discussion with practising coordinators, teachers, OFSTED inspectors, advisers and teacher-educators in search of what they feel is good practice and the essential skills necessary for both the subject and its coordination in school. Throughout this research process I became much more aware of the role of the coordinator, about what practices do and do not work and the constraints and pressures facing primary teachers who are faced with the demanding task of being a class teacher and a coordinator; all of this usually with ever-diminishing resources.

This data is integrated throughout the book in the form of interview transcripts and case study materials. All of the case study materials are drawn from four different schools, which range from a large urban, multicultural school to a small primary school (each has been given a pseudonym). Even though your school may not have the same characteristics I am sure you will still find the materials relevant. Some of the material is used as *exemplars* of how things are done e.g. sample policies. Alternatively the material is presented for *reflection*, asking you to consider specific issues, make comparisons. It is all related to a series of tasks which are presented throughout the book.

How the book works

You may decide to read the book chapter by chapter or dip into different parts depending on your individual preference and needs. Whichever way you chose, I hope it makes sense, is realistic and will help you reflect not only on your role as a coordinator but also on the role of physical education in the school curriculum.

Part One begins with some general information on understanding your role, recognising and developing personal management skills with a particular emphasis on evaluation and development in Chapter 3. This leads into Part Two which addresses more specific aspects of physical education, knowing your subject, the National Curriculum requirements and general leading principles relating to 'good practice'. Chapter 5, addresses effective teaching and learning in PE and focuses on creating a positive learning environment for children. This is expanded in Chapter 6, which specifically looks at securing a 'safe' environment.

Part Three, planning subject documentation, commences with planning a whole school policy for PE. It encourages you to look at what you already do and evaluate your policies in relation to good practice and external expectations. I recognise throughout that this is not something you can do alone; it is a whole school responsibility that you coordinate. Fulfilling your role will involve governors, the headteacher, all staff and pupils. Getting things written down is one of the most difficult tasks, modifying it is relatively easy as long as you are prepared for people to challenge existing documents or first drafts. This chapter recognises the importance of sharing ideas, not only with your own colleagues but others in partner schools, working with LEA and HE colleagues. This moves us to working in partnership which should help maximise the use of resources both human and material, in order to increase opportunities for the pupils and staff. Chapter 8 looks at the implementation of your policies through a scheme of work, units of work and lesson planning.

Monitoring pupil achievement is an integral part of teaching and learning. The complex process of how this can be successfully achieved in PE is addressed in Part Four, where Chapter 9 specifically focuses on the what, why and how of assessment.

Whatever we do in schools is linked with resources and the final part looks at managing resources. PE budgets are usually limited, smaller than other subject budgets, and by its very nature the subject requirements can be expensive. As coordinator you will need to know who sells what, how much it costs, and link subject development plans with your budget.

Part one

The role of the PE coordinator

Chapter 1

What does being a PE coordinator involve?

The class teacher has always been seen at the very heart of British primary education (Harrison and Theaker, 1989; Wragg, 1993; McNamara, 1994). However, an explosion of knowledge in both traditional and new subjects, the use of computers, cross-curricular themes such as health and safety, and the development of personal transferable skills, have all contributed to increasing the complexity of the primary school curriculum. This, coupled with society's expectations, have made it difficult, if not impossible, for the class teacher to keep up to date. The idea that primary teachers need support no longer seems to be in doubt and the value of delegating curriculum responsibility to subject coordinators has gained momentum as one way of offering this support. In 1986 the House of Commons Select Committee endorsed the role of coordinators in curriculum management and school development. It would appear that there is no longer a place for a teacher whose sole responsibility is his or her class.

By 1989 all initial teacher education courses in England and Wales had to prepare primary training students to be ready, when qualified, to take on the role of leading other teaching staff in a specialist subject area. What a challenge! This was also recognised by the Department of Education and Science (DFE)

❛ *To meet the requirements of the National Curriculum, and the need for more systematic coverage of all subjects in all classes, many schools now find it helpful to identify 'co-ordinators' with strengths in particular subjects who can assist and help train staff.* (DFE, 1995, Circular 14/93)

Most recently the Teacher Training Agency (TTA) proposals for a qualification for subject leaders recognised different sources of evidence that has shown

❝ *. . . pupil achievement is higher when the role of the subject leader is clearly identified and effectively implemented. Effective leaders make a major contribution to improving schools and raising the levels of pupil achievement.* (1996, p. 4)

Extensive work by researchers such as Holly and Southworth (1989), Day, Whitaker and Johnson (1990), Alexander, Rose and Woodhead (1992), Day and Norman (1993), Davies (1995) and Harrison (1995) have all contributed to improving our understanding about the role of subject coordinators. This new 'middle' management role has become firmly established in the primary school. But who are these coordinators? What are they expected to do?

This chapter will address the role of the PE coordinator, sometimes referred to in other documents as subject managers or subject leaders, and offer guidance on what is recognised as good practice. Many of the skills discussed are generic and common to all subject areas. The subject specific advice is based on my own experiences and research into existing practice promoted by colleagues with varied levels of experience. Throughout the research process I was keen to identify not only what coordinators are required to do in terms of their job specification, but what they felt they ought to do and how.

What type of person is the coordinator?

Over a period of four weeks I analysed sixty-six *Times Educational Supplement* advertisements, and fifteen follow-up job descriptions for coordinators. It became evident that the emphasis placed on certain qualities varies considerably from school to school. The most popular expectations can be summarised in a few extracts:

The Governors of this expanding first and middle school
are seeking to appoint a highly motivated, experienced and
enthusiastic teacher with an ability to lead a Year 6 team of
5 classes.
The successful applicant will be a member of the managment
team having personal responsibility for the co-ordination of
physical education throughout the school.

An enthusiastic and energetic professional with . . .
experience across the primary phase,
excellent class teacher skills,
ability to work co-operatively as part of a team
. . . is required for this large multicultural primary school.

We require a suitably qualified, experienced and enthusiastic
teacher
initially for Year 4, who is able to co-ordinate the P.E. and P.S.H.E.
work throughout the school.

'Experience' appeared in 90 per cent of the advertisements and
was the most frequently mentioned quality, with 'enthusiasm'
including 'highly motivated' following closely behind. This
is not surprising information if coordinators are to be
responsible for

❝ *. . . raising standards of achievement and be able to demon-*
   strate excellent teaching and interpersonal skills . . .

❝ *. . . leading curriculum development . . .*

❝ *. . . to lead colleagues . . .*

This is not to ignore 'sense of humour', 'vision', 'reliable',
'innovative', 'able to raise standards', 'organisational and
managerial skills', 'good class teacher', 'commitment to after
school clubs', 'equal opportunities' and 'integration of SEN
pupils'. This data also identifies the range of responsibilities
and the type of environment that coordinators will be working
in. No two schools are the same.

What is certain is that being a coordinator involves a great
deal more than being a good class teacher. You can be an

excellent classroom teacher yet a poor coordinator. Your skills in the classroom may be what earns you the respect of your colleagues and contributes to your promotion, but you will need some new and different skills to succeed as a coordinator. These 'skills' will be addressed throughout various chapters of this book.

The responsibilities associated with being subject co-ordinator are described in many ways. Any job description should include

- a statement of intent;
- a reference to how the role fits in to school policy and management;
- a list of areas of responsibility, general and specific;
- the process of review.

The third area listed above might include: review of policy; reporting to staff, head and governors; development of continuity and progression; differentiation and access; assessment, recording and reporting; ordering and managing resources; liaison with outside agencies. The key skills, roles and responsibilities will be determined by the school needs and authority within which you work. This was confirmed by Webb (1994) whose research showed that 'the amount and nature of the work fulfilled by co-ordinators varied enormously from school to school, and often between co-ordinators in the same school' (para. 5.9) The exact duties a PE coordinator will be asked to perform and the expectations made of an NQT will differ from those made on a more experienced teacher. At least, this is how it should work in practice!

Understanding the role of the coordinator

You will need to have a clear understanding of what your job as a coordinator involves in your school. It will be easier for you if your colleagues also have a clear understanding of the more general role of subject leaders and how they feature in the management of the school. The current school inspection framework reports on leadership and management and

6 *. . . how well staff with management responsibilities contribute to the quality of education provided.* (OFSTED, 1995, p. 100)

Suggestion

Do you have a job description? What does it say?
This is the first thing to look at. It should outline what is expected of you and will give you a guide as to how the role of the PE coordinator is viewed in your school. How does it relate to the areas identified above?

They claim that in a well-managed school, responsibilities are clearly defined, there is effective delegation and staff understand the role they are encouraged to play in the development and running of the school (p. 101). A useful starting point is to look at whether job descriptions are clear and realistic and the extent to which staff understand and are committed to them. Look at the following descriptions. They clearly identify areas of responsibility. How do they relate to your own description? Do you need more detail in your own description?

Job description for Woodstock Primary School — PE Coordinator
The duties of the PE coordinator will involve:
- keeping up to date with best practice in physical education teaching and the national and local curriculums;
- monitoring of the school's physical education policy and updating this where necessary;
- auditing, ordering and taking care of the school's physical education resources;
- arranging staff development, INSET or focused discussions on agreed practices;
- talking to the governors and advisers about the school's physical education teaching;
- attending courses provided by the LEA or Higher Education Institute.

Job description for Avondale Primary School — PE Coordinator
The main responsibilities are:
- to take responsibility for managing the subject in the school as delegated through the headteacher;
- to organise and monitor learning in PE, not only what children are learning but why and how they are learning it;
- to work with staff, teaching and non teaching to help them develop their skills, knowledge and understanding of the subject and how it can be taught so that children's learning is at the focus of their work;
- to offer advice and guidance on standards of achievement and the assessment of pupil learning;
- to facilitate the coordination of resources;
- to highlight links with other subjects on the curriculum also with other agencies in the community and how to maximise learning opportunities;
- to support teachers' ongoing professional development.

Both job descriptions tell us what the headteacher expects from the coordinator. But not all descriptions are as helpful. During an interview one co-ordinator outlined her job in much broader terms:

❝ *When I was appointed I was told that I was coordinator for PE and that was that.* (HC)

She went on to say that she received a one-day induction course and was then left to her own devices; 'learning on the job' was very much her responsibility.

You need to be clear about *what you are expected to do* and this will involve talking to the headteacher and negotiating a detailed description.

The TTA (1996) description for a subject leader will provide you with a useful comparative framework. There are five key areas of responsibility:

■ Teaching, Learning and the Curriculum
■ Monitoring, Evaluating and Improving
■ People and Relationships
■ Managing Resources
■ Accountability (pp. 5–7)

How to negotiate your job description

1 Book an appointment with the Head or Deputy.
2 Use your written job description as a basis for discussion and be prepared for an open exchange of views.
3 Know what you want to say:
   ■ State your needs and views clearly, e.g. 'I'd like to clarify my responsibility for the ordering of equipment, maintenance of facilities'.
   ■ Try to keep calm.
   ■ Focus on issues.
   ■ Make notes.
4 Clarify what the school wants or needs. What would you like me to do? What do you see as the main priorities? It may be helpful to divide aims or priorities into 'termly blocks' to make the overview easier to manage. If there are key events such as a school sports day will time and resources be made available to facilitate the running and organisation of the day?

5 Try to understand both views. You need to appreciate the Head's view while at the same time expressing your own. *'I appreciate your . . . but. . . .' 'I do realise there are difficulties here but. . . .'*
6 Be prepared to take a decision.
7 Be assertive.

What happens if a Head's behaviour is aggressive? or difficult? The best approach is to make a statement about the effect this is having on you. This is the strongest form of assertive behaviour and is only to be used when absolutely necessary. *'You don't seem to be listening to what I'm saying and it's not helping our discussion. You are raising your voice and it is making us both . . .'*

This type of meeting with your Head is an integral part of your role in managing people. Chapter 2 deals in more detail with the idea of managing people in difficult situations in an assertive way.

What does the role involve?

Being a good PE coordinator will not only involve keeping up to date with good practice in PE, but also what is good practice in management and leadership. This information is offered by many of the professional associations and organisations involved in physical education. For example, the Physical Education Association of United Kingdom (PEAUK) and the British Association of Advisers and Lecturers in Physical Education (BAALPE). The introduction of OFSTED and an increase in research into primary PE has also made it easier for coordinators to gain an insight into what their role involves and what it is that makes good practice. The following extracts featured in the OFSTED report on *Physical Education and Sport in School: A Survey of Good Practice* give us some ideas (it was based on a survey of 86 selected primary, secondary and special schools):

■ Management of PE was good when staff worked as a team, in that values and policies were shared and implemented.
■ Good departments had clear documentation laying out logical rationale for PE, objectives were pursued

Suggestion

Divide your job into main areas of responsibility. What is realistic? Further negotiation with the headteacher may be necessary to help you prioritise and approach your work in a realistic way. You may also want to seek the views of your colleagues: what do they see as the most important needs in PE? Time is always difficult to find in a busy school, but see if part of a staff meeting can be allocated for this or prepare a questionnaire for the staff to take away and do in their own time. Revisit the headteacher and discuss your proposals for a way forward (this will be similar to developing a development or action plan, to be discussed in Chapter 3). Once you have agreed on a way forward, present this to your colleagues via a staff meeting or a brief summary paper.

purposefully with procedures and practices monitored systematically.

■ Regular meetings ensured subject review and generated open-mindedness.

■ There was concern for efficient management of time, staffing, resources and accommodation and this promoted high standards of concern to staff, pupils and parents.

■ Specific points about primary provision identified the importance of the headteachers and the need for this person to be enthusiastic and supportive.

■ OFSTED reported good subject coordinators as confident and knowledgable about the subject.

■ Successful schools had a clear policy for PE, with established routines particularly for dress and the handling of apparatus.

■ The effective subject coordinator, with support from the headteacher and other staff, had produced an overall scheme of work. This took account of the different stages of development of primary children and ensured consistent practice over the two of key stages primary schooling.

■ This corporate planning made possible the continuous development of learning between classes and year groups and avoided fragmentation of learning.

■ The principles underpinning the programme of work were understood and shared by all staff, who had high expectations of pupils. (OFSTED, 1995, p. 4)

This long list might appear quite daunting at first but you can begin to tackle it in a systematic way. A new coordinator cannot be expected to do everything at once and managing your own job will be one of your first responsibilities. Consider it to be a developmental process, one of the first stages of which is to analyse your agreed job description and set out a series of priorities.

Coordinator — specialist or generalist?

There is ongoing debate about the role of the coordinator as a generalist or specialist, particularly at Key Stage 2.

Most teachers and some nursery assistants hold responsibility for aspects of the school's curriculum and organisation and

some hold more than one, without necessarily having special-
ist expertise.   (OFSTED, 1995, p. 101)

This is an important issue as it will affect the nature of your
role and responsibilities. What is your school policy? What
are the roles and responsibilities of other coordinators in the
school? Has the school had a PE coordinator before? The
critical question for physical education across the primary
school is the breadth of the curriculum and the relation of Key
Stage 1 to Key Stage 2 to Key Stage 3. To what extent can
teachers have expertise over such a wide field? It is safe to
assume that some teachers will find this breadth a challenge.
How much will you be expected to assist, support and lead?
Is your role as generalist teacher acting as a coordinator, or
is it a generalist/consultant, or is it a specialist?

Many colleagues will expect you to be an *expert* in PE. They
will expect you to have the *knowledge* and *understanding* to
demystify some of the PE jargon. Teachers will naturally look
to you for guidance and assistance to help them deliver the
goods. The coordinator should therefore consider three things
in relation to knowledge.

■ *Assess your own knowledge.* How much do you know
  about PE? What personal philosophy do you hold? At the
  outset you will inevitably have strengths and weaknesses.
  Acknowledge these. Don't pretend to be an expert at
  something you're not. Be honest, but avoid sitting back
  and waiting for your weaknesses to disappear.
■ *Develop your knowledge.* Regularly review and up date your
  knowledge through personal appraisal, links with other
  coordinators and via professional organisations. Seek advice
  and look to colleagues to help you address these weaker
  areas and help others to do the same. If colleagues see that
  you are willing to have a go, this may well rub off on them.
  Leading by example is the best way forward.
■ *Share your knowledge* with colleagues in a supportive
  professional way.

A solid knowledge base will provide a firm foundation for all
the work involved in being a good coordinator. It must be
recognised, however, that most teachers leave initial teacher
education having received very basic courses in physical

education. This is further complicated by the fact that many teachers become PE coordinators because they are 'enthusiastic, young, fit and healthy' not always because they have a depth of PE knowledge.

As mentioned earlier, most job advertisements look for an experienced teacher with expertise. This differs from reality where the majority of PE coordinators tend to be inexperienced recruits to the profession with limited background in main subject PE. A summary of results from 56 replies from a survey of 100 schools revealed that 51 per cent of the PE coordinators were unpromoted class teachers; 29 per cent had another subject; and 21 per cent shared the role with another teacher (Harrison, 1996). In reality the experience of PE coordinators is limited and this must influence their knowledge base.

Summary
- Be aware of your job description via consultation with the headteacher.
- Formulate areas of priority according to what the head and you agree on.
- Lead by example.
- Share ideas and involve colleagues.

Chapter 2   Developing management skills

As well as being a subject expert, the coordinator will be expected to do 'management' work. The different chapters in this book are designed not only to develop your subject knowledge but also your knowledge of management, what it means and what it involves, so as to help you develop your coordination skills.

As a coordinator, you will be seen as middle management and, we must remind ourselves, this involves more than just being a good teacher. Management work is something that education has resisted for many years, believing that it belonged to the world of industry. More recently it has received systematic analysis and the principles of good management are recognised as inherent in all teachers' work. But what does this mean?

Definitions of management are so many and varied that this book could be dedicated to this subject alone. My approach is to be practical and offer a general overview. Kemp and Nathan (1989) describe management as:

■ The setting of overall objectives, the formulation of policy and plans designed to achieve these objectives, and the establishment of standards for measuring the activity that puts people, money and machines to work in the production of goods and services.

■ The planning and oversight of the activities of an organisation (i.e. the school) in relation to its goals, procedures and the tasks of its personnel (i.e. the staff).

■ The totality of executive control, i.e. planning, coordination, leadership and evaluation.
■ Getting things done through people, with the most effective use of all the available resources.

Similarly, Everard and Morris (1990) consider management in its broadest sense is about:

1 setting direction, aims and objectives;
2 planning how progress will be made or a goal achieved;
3 organising available resources (people, time, materials) so that the goal can be economically achieved in a planned way;
4 controlling the process (i.e. measuring achievement against plan and taking corrective action where appropriate);
5 setting and improving organisational standards. (p. 4)

This definition uses some of the language taken from industry and commerce but the essence of the work is applicable to education. Both definitions relate to the role of the coordinator and the type of work identified in the job descriptions and the OFSTED recognition of good practice. In many ways one could argue that every teacher is a manager. It is evident that to manage well you have to be able to

■ **manage yourself** — e.g. be a good role model; manage administration and time; provide leadership;
■ **manage people** — e.g. know your colleagues; teamwork; delegation; management styles; communication skills;
■ **manage the subject** — e.g. curriuculum planning, implementation, and evaluation; managing resources.

These are not to be considered separate aspects of management work but recognised as interrelated areas.

All things considered, management is about getting things done and effective management is about teamwork and shared leadership (Day, Johnston and Whitaker, 1985, p. 26). That is, it is not about a named individual but about the function of a group as a whole. They claim that

❛ *The kind of management structure more likely to be success-ful in meeting the challenges of the future is one that makes optimum use of the human resources at its disposal. This will*

> *not only require the skilled combining of individual strengths and abilities but a capacity to build group and partnership skills within the working team.*　　　　　(1985, p. 29)

The work of Torrington and Weightman (1991) and Peters and Waterman (1988) all endorse this collaborative style of management as the most efficient and effective. Harrison (1995) suggests it is also worth taking notice of the 'culture of management' you will find in your school. The importance of understanding this culture 'the way we do things and relate to each other around here' (Fullan and Hargreaves, 1992) will recur throughout the text. It relates to the ethos created by those who live and breathe in your school. Such a structure is easier to conceive than it is to achieve in practice. Part of your role will be to contribute to this culture by managing others in such a way as to develop a team/whole school approach to physical education.

Management requires a number of skills and personal qualities. Those identified by the TTA are shown below.

Subject Leaders should be able to:
- (i)　express and instil clear educational values;
- (ii)　motivate and inspire pupils, staff, parents, governors and the wider community;
- (iii)　anticipate problems, collect and weigh evidence, make judgments and take descisions;
- (iv)　adapt to changing circumstances and new ideas;
- (v)　solve problems and identify opportunities;
- (vi)　negotiate, delegate, consult, direct and operate as part of a team;
- (vii)　follow through and pursue policies to implementation, and monitor and review their effectiveness in practice;
- (viii)　communicate effectively, both verbally and in writing, with staff at all levels, pupils, parents, governors and the wider community;
- (ix)　identify, analyse and interpret current educational management and research issues relating to the subject and discern their relevance to the school;
- (x)　recognise and use the most appropriate management strategy for each situation;
- (xi)　deal sensitively with people, resolve conflicts and, where appropriate, build consensus;

(xii) understand and intepret statistics, financial information and other data;

(xiii) seek advice and support as appropriate;

(xiv) prioritise and manage their own time; and

(xv) maximise the use of information technology for curriculum and administrative purposes.

(TTA, 1996, p. 13)

Managing yourself

Managing yourself is crucial if you are to do a good job, so you need to ask yourself some important questions. How well do you know yourself? Do you have the necessary skills? Look at the skills collated under the last task. How many do you have? What qualities are you looking to develop? How well do these match with the TTA outline on p. 19. What exactly does the role of the PE co-ordinator involve in your school? What are your strengths? What types of jobs do you like doing? What are your weaknesses? Is there anything that you don't like doing? You will need to understand your own management competence and know the areas in need of further development.

Being a good role model

Your role as coordinator will inevitably involve you in taking responsibility for other people. Colleagues will see you as a role model in PE. They will look to you for guidance and support so it is crucial that you:

■ lead by example;

■ develop and refine your own good practice.

Managing administration

The job of subject coordinator involves managing the operation of the subject and this inevitably means carrying out a range of administrative tasks. These vary from organising the overall subject documentation and the preparation of policies and a

PE handbook, to day-to-day tasks related to teaching PE, to organising the whole school special PE activities such as sports days, school teams, not to mention dealing with the miscellaneous paperwork that finds its way into your pigeon-hole. The difficulty for you is that you will have to spend most of your working time doing something else — teaching pupils — so what little time you will have, will need to be carefully planned with priorities clearly identified. Some tips on how to streamline some of the paperwork are provided as examples in the next section.

Time management — time to do the job

Time for you to do the work of the subject coordinator is crucial but will undoubtedly be limited. One of your first tasks as coordinator must be to discuss with the headteacher how much time you will be allocated to do the job. Time can be made available through part-time or floating cover, supply and peripatetic teacher cover, working with student-teachers, exchange and doubling up classes, all of these possibilities need to be considered. In small schools it may be virtually impossible to secure non-contact time.

Given that demands on teachers are forever increasing and coordinating PE will involve time and energy, you will need to make some conscious decisions about how much time you can spend on different aspects of your workload. Consider how much personal time you need to devote to the role and how much to your class. Both you and your headteacher need to recognise that you cannot to everything at once.

Making good use of time involves:
- Thinking;
- Planning ahead — anticipating;
- Establishing priorities — what is urgent (e.g. in terms of school needs or SDP aims) and what is important (e.g. in terms of NC coverage);
- Being ruthless, realistic and resisting distraction;
- Learning to say 'no'.

FIG 2.1
Dealing with the paperwork

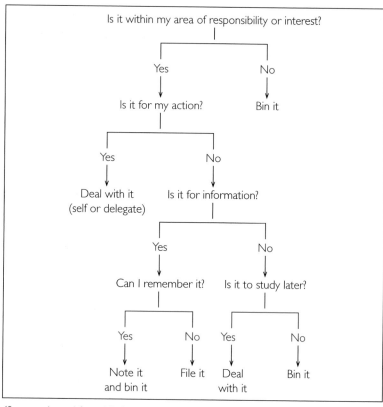

(*Source*: adapted from Nathan and Kemp, 1989, p. 38. Reproduced with the permission of Stanley Thornes Publishers Ltd from *Middle Management in Schools: A Survival Guide*, first published in 1989.)

Making the time you need is a personal challenge for all coordinators. Here are some pointers that I have found useful:

■ Try and make a regular time slot for dealing with routine matters; for example 15 minutes at the start of each day or 20/30 minutes at the start of every other day.
■ Avoid going to your pigeon-hole every time you go into the staffroom. Clear it just once a day or even every other day.
■ Be realistic about how much time you can allocate to a task.
■ Try to take a decision on paperwork the first time it comes into your hands. Deal with it, then bin or file it! Try to handle paper just once (see Figure 2.1).
■ Develop your IT skills (in your spare time).

Time-management techniques such as preparing an annual calendar of jobs to do, weekly action planning, keeping a diary and project planning are recommended by Everard and Morris (1990) and Chedzoy (1996). This area is discussed further in the section on monitoring and evaluation (pp. 38–59).

Long-term good time management involves taking stock of your responsibilities, conducting an audit of PE provision and preparing a development plan with short-, mid- and long-term objectives.

Leadership

The job descriptions on pages 11–12 remind us that the coordinator's role is concerned with people as well as tasks. As subject coordinator you will be responsible for getting others moving, or keeping them moving in the desired direction (Clerkin, 1990, p. 23). This will involve people skills, or interpersonal skills, and these will define your relationships with other people.

Leadership, like management, is judged by results, the emphasis is placed on behaviour rather than plans and policies, and should be seen in terms of the function of the staff. It is not the responsibility of one member of staff. Leadership involves effective teamwork, where leaders emerge in response to different situations. Teachers hold personal qualities which can be closely related to successful learning in pupils. The same qualities are likely to contribute to group cohesion, effective teamwork and collaborative management.

The complexity of the leadership role is recognised later in this chapter, where a continuum of leadership behaviour encourages you to develop a range of leadership behaviours as an integral part of your management style. Effective leadership is a result of a complex interaction between style, classroom cultures, uses and perceptions of power and authority, and individual and group relationships as applied to particular tasks.

Managing people

The ability to develop a whole school approach to teaching PE is important and calls on your ability to get on well with your colleagues. In their book on *Leadership and Curriculum in the Primary School*, Day, Hall, Gammage and Coles (1993) talk about making people a priority. It will be largely up to you to create and maintain an atmosphere in which people are willing and motivated to work with a sense of purpose in physical education. In this section I focus on some general points about managing people.

Know your colleagues

On page 19, I made reference to understanding the culture and ethos of your school. How well do you know your colleagues? Take time to get to know people's skills and experience. This may involve:

- having informal chats in the staffroom during lunchtimes, etc.;
- finding out about individual staff responsibilities;
- attending formal school activities;
- attending social activities.

This knowledge will help you to know what you can expect from your colleagues, and gives you an indication of where they might need help and support. Taking an interest in people as professionals will encourage collegiality and help promote a good whole school ethos.

Get to know what different people think about PE. Remember that among the many PE enthusiasts, you will have primary colleagues who are reluctant PE participants. They will recall horror stories of their own unhappy experiences. They will have had limited training, and the unique organisational setting, large open spaces and ever-changing weather conditions contribute to their negative images of the subject and their lack of confidence and competence. While physical education is firmly established as a foundation subject, Sanderson (1995) believes you may find that in practice it has rarely been given a great deal of attention by some teachers. She acknowledges the huge demands on primary teachers but comments,

> *. . . despite the Dearing reforms, . . . there may also be a genuine lack of interest in the area for, traditionally, PE has not been taken seriously in the primary school. Too often it is regarded as an interruption in the serious business of the school day and little more than playtime.* (p. 172)

With this is mind your role as coordinator for PE is clearly a crucial and challenging one if the subject is to have a positive image in school. You have a responsibility to try and understand colleagues' strengths and concerns, listen to their worries, share experiences and offer support as appropriate. Some people talk about 'Positive stroking': giving praise and thanks, showing colleagues the work they are doing is appreciated. It makes people feel valued and helps build teamwork and support. Knowing what colleagues think will help you understand them and their image of the subject. (You may need to recruit the support of the headteacher to overcome any steadfast barriers to PE: suggestions on how to manage conflict situations are discussed on page 35.)

Teamwork — sharing

The kind of management structure most likely to be successful in meeting the challenges facing all those involved in education is one that makes optimum use of the human resources at its disposal. Frisby (1994) believes

> *The effective school is one where the whole is greater than the sum of its parts. Given that the most powerful resource, and the most expensive, is the expertise of its teachers, the most effective school is the one which can combine these individual talents and keep them working towards commonly agreed goals.*
>
> (p. 75)

The so-called WAR report (DES, 1992) advises that 'policies should emerge from collective staff discussion' (p. 158) and 'the development of shared educational beliefs' (p. 156). This will not only require combining individual strengths and abilities, but a capacity to build group and partnership skills within the working team. By working as a team, involving team members in management and decision-making you will encourage a feeling of ownership and willingness to participate in the changes that will ultimately take shape. This level of team involvement is considered to be as crucial as

> *. . . people are best motivated to work towards goals that they have been involved in setting and to which they therefore feel committed.*
>
> (Everard and Morris, 1990, p. 24)

Teamwork means sharing talents, expertise and problems. Although it is not always easy, involving colleagues and tackling any problems and issues collectively as they emerge will help you work towards establishing a collegiate approach in your school. For example, many tasks involving group decision making all contribute to creating effective teamwork; a few examples are included here.

Establishing a school ethos depends on the creation of agreed and shared PE aims. During staff development workshop it will be useful to:

- Brainstorm what you consider to be the main aims of PE for your school. (Sometimes it is necessary to have these aims prepared so as to ensure coverage following a brainstorm activity.)
- Agree on which activities can best meet these aims.

Developing a school policy in PE using team/whole school decision-making:

1 Designing a policy for 'Safe handling of gymnastics apparatus'
Set colleagues a task to identify key issues related to using equipment, e.g. finding out about NC requirements for children using apparatus; good practice of taking out, placing and putting away of apparatus; BAALPE guidance. Collate the key issues and put them into some sort of rank order:

SAFE HANDLING OF APPARATUS
- Show the class how to carry and manoeuvre each piece of apparatus.
- Show them where and how to grip each piece of apparatus.
- Show them how to lift the apparatus and which way to face as they carry it.
- Show the class how to place the apparatus safely on the ground.

---

2 Designing an assessment policy in PE
During my discussions with colleagues it became evident that any form of assessment in primary education can be difficult as some staff view it as quite threatening. This is because once a descision or assessment has been made, they fear the next step — 'What now?' In PE many teachers do not have a clear or confident approach, and will worry about attempting any form of assessment. They know assessment underpins learning, may influence their delivery, content or approach, but they are usually happy to be controlling the children in what they consider to be an 'alien

environment'. Designing an assessment policy therefore needs careful decision-making on your part. The guidelines offered in Figure 2.2 have been successfully used by coordinators in Hereford and Worcester.

Delegation

To do the coordinators' job well, one thing is certain — you can't do everything yourself. The art of delegation is important, generating an atmosphere of sharing within your team will help to promote understanding and an appreciation that working together maximises resources and makes the best use of individuals' strengths. As Harrison and Theaker (1989) concluded

❝ . . . a great deal of enthusiasm and expertise in specific cur-riculum has been locked into individual classrooms. It is only when we share knowledge and skills that the true potential of the professional teacher is realised. (p. 5)

Getting colleagues to volunteer is the secret to success, but not all respond to this and need persuasion and cajoling — they need managing!

Management styles

During my early experience of managing colleagues I soon discovered that my skills of leading pupils in the classroom were not instantly transferable to leading teachers in the staffroom. Managing adults, teachers and colleagues, as you are no doubt aware, is quite different. It is often seen as secondary to the task of getting on with the job of teaching in the classroom. Skills are transferable, however, and as you use different teaching styles with your pupils so you will use different management styles with colleagues. You will need to consider colleagues' varying experiences, values and attitudes, not to mention their personalities and preferences. Styles of management and leadership vary from the autocratic, 'I'm the boss so you'll do as I say', to the more democratic, 'Let's agree

FIG 2.2

An example of decision making and assessment in PE at Key Stages 1 and 2

STAGE 1	
What is the decision intended to achieve?	Formulation of an agreed policy on assessment of pupil attainment in physical education at Key Stage 1 and 2.
By when must it be taken?	July 1997.
What constraints are there?	Limited knowledge and resources pertaining to assessment.
What further information do you require?	Example of assessment criteria methods, records.
STAGE 2	
Who is to participate in the decision making?	All staff teaching physical education: school's assessment coordinator.
Is everyone appropriately briefed?	Discussion at previous physical education related meetings.
Has a date been set for concluding the process?	May 1997.
What strategies are to be used in reaching a decision?	Open discussion on basic principles, evaluation of exemplar material, vote on appropriate methods and extent of pilot project.
STAGE 3	
What relevant information is available?	Exemplars; results of INSET; advice from PE support team.
Can you list all the options open to you?	Formative; summative; NC-based criterion referenced; norm referenced; LEA assessment model.
What consequences will you follow from each option?	Pros and cons of each type of assessment noted during discussions.
What strategy can help you make a decision?	Pilot scheme using formative progressive statements from NC
STAGE 4	
How do you plan to implement the decision?	Pilot scheme review and evaluation.
Have you briefed everyone affected by it?	Headteacher; all teachers of Key Stages 1 and 2.

(*Source*: Hereford and Worcester Curriculum Guidelines 1992)

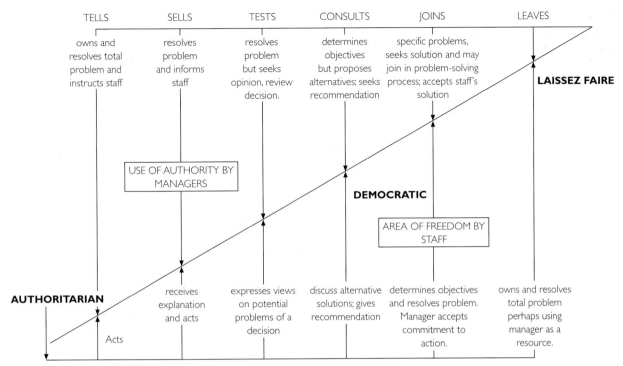

(*Source*: Kemp and and Nathan, 1989, p. 109. Reproduced with permission of Stanley Thornes Publishers Ltd from *Middle Management in Schools: A Survival Guide*, first published in 1989.)

FIG 2.3
The continuum of leadership behaviour

the most appropriate way forward'. Figure 2.3, illustrates a continuum of management and leadership behaviour presented by Kemp and Nathan (1989, p. 109).

The style you use will depend upon the situation and the people involved. Moving in and out of different styles is the secret to interactive management. Your knowledge about your colleagues will help you chose the right style. It is no good giving in to people who are steadfast on principles, when ultimately you have no choice but to make a decision and move forward. It is your job to monitor colleagues' reactions, listen to others and endeavour to guide them as and when you feel appropriate. Management style is one of the single biggest factors in making quality improvements in schools. Whatever style you adopt, it is important that you understand that good management is about *getting things done* (Day, Johnston and Whitaker, 1985, p. 26).

Suggestion

To consider leadership styles. Look at the continuum of leadership behaviour in Figure 2.3. What styles of leadership do you use? Which style of management do you feel most comfortable with? Is it effective in all situations?

Communication

Developing a whole school approach to PE will rely on good communication between you and your colleagues. In addition you will at times need to communicate with colleagues from other schools, as well as governors, parents, members of the community, advisers, consultants and even OFSTED. Good communication allows us to both give out and gather information, including knowledge and instructions. It allows us to support, motivate and to facilitate each other. It is also the main means of influencing peoples' behaviour. Yet, often people are too busy to communicate effectively. Following a research study into primary provision, Jack (1995) reported:

> *One of the most powerful issues which manifested itself strongly throughout my work was the apparent lack of communication between the headteacher, PE curriculum leader and general teaching staff, resulting in confusion as to what each person expected of the other.* (p. 5)

We need to learn from this research and begin to realise that even though communication is a natural activity, *good* communication is a complex skill which can take a variety of forms:

- Formal — your school may have an established system for passing on information, e.g. school bulletin, meetings.
- Informal — personal contacts during everyday business.
- Upwards/downwards/sideways — information and ideas need to be communicated through the school's managerial hierarchy and to all colleagues involved in delivering PE.
- Oral — in meetings, at interviews, in informal talks.
- Written — memos, letters, subject documentation and reports.

To keep communication effective, you will need to use a mixture of these forms, according to the purpose and situation.

As a coordinator, some colleagues will expect you to take the lead, do the talking, be able to articulate your views, argue a point, motivate and keep them informed. But being a good listener is equally important: this involves taking notice of colleagues' views and their reactions to feedback, and knowing

Suggestion

Think about your vision for PE in your school. How do you set about communicating this to others?

what's going on. Good communication has to be an active two-way process if you are to set the right type of atmosphere. How do you encourage colleagues to communicate with you? Are you approachable? Do you set time aside when colleagues can chat with you, formally or informally about PE; their ideas, problems etc.? Are you able to talk about PE at a level which your colleagues understand and feel comfortable with? Do you approach and consult colleagues, and involve them in PE business?

Good communication means the subject is running smoothly, without too much fuss because everyone is aware of what is going on. Staff will feel comfortable to talk to you about any problems. If you take time to communicate with your colleagues it can also help to increase the 'visibility' and 'image' of PE in your school. As a coordinator your own reputation and the reputation of the subject will be closely linked to the 'image' you create. Of course this does also depend on colleagues and how they react but you need to carefully shape the image that you want other people to have of you and your subject. Your subject image is communicated via your documentation, school prospectus, policies, syllabus, working papers as well as notice boards and memos.

Improving your communication. How often do you think about the way you communicate? Do you know the forms of communication your colleagues prefer? Do you present the right message or can it be misinterpreted? How often have you heard colleagues say:
> 'Thanks for letting me know so soon . . .'
> 'Nobody ever tells me anything . . . !'
> 'Why are we always the last to know . . .'
> 'Oh no, not another memo . . .'

Listen to what they say. What suggestions can they offer? Making sure everyone knows what they need to know at the right time is an essential part of effective management.

Suggestion

Understanding the classic mistakes of poor meetings. Think about some of the meetings that you have felt were a waste of time. Make a list of the most obvious mistakes. How does your list compare with the classic mistakes listed in Figure 2.4?

Meetings

At times you will be expected to organise and chair meetings. These can be whole school or small group affairs, formal and informal. Meetings can also be short, personal and private.

	Classic Mistakes	**Some Pointers**
The day and timing	■ Was it really a good idea to have a meeting on a day when it was the last day for the completion of school reports. ■ Are 3 hour meetings after a busy day at school reasonable? ■ Is Friday after school a good night for policy making?	■ Pick a day when everyone who needs to attend can. ■ A regular meeting slot and good notice can help overcome any problems. ■ Get the number of meetings right: not too many; not too few.
Agenda	■ Is 15 items on an agenda too many?	■ If it is to be helpful in running a meeting an agenda needs to be more than a list. It needs to be developmental.
Papers	■ Last minute circulation of papers leaving limited time for staff to think about issues etc.	■ Always prepare these well in advance and circulate them to all colleagues.
Venue	■ Classroom with rows of desks formally set out.	■ How the room is organised can influence the discussion. Think carefully about the style and organise any resources beforehand.
Chairing the meeting	■ Ill-informed and lack of awareness of how to involve different people. ■ Little leadership.	■ This involves being both a referee and a leader. Try to be flexible and keep the meeting focused on the business in hand.
Decision making	■ No summary of discussions and no decisions made. ■ A feeling of not having achieved any business.	■ Anticipate difficulties. Consider all arguments. Know how far you are able to compromise if it gets tough.

Source: adapted from Nathan and Kemp, 1989, pp. 89–91. Reproduced with the permission of Stanley Thornes Publishers Ltd from *Middle Management in Schools: A Survival Guide*, first published in 1989.)

FIG 2.4
Avoiding poor meetings

Meetings are one of the key forms of communication and are the most common method used to pass on information, discuss issues openly and make decisions together. They are crucial in coordinating effort and effecting change. But we all know that some meetings can be a waste of time, they can leave colleagues feeling frustrated and occasionally confused.

Organising meetings
Poorly conducted meetings produce bad feeling and are an ineffective use of precious time. Whenever you assume responsibility for the management of a meeting consider the following points:

Skills for effective meetings
1 Be businesslike
2 Communicate clearly
3 Listen carefully
4 Keep focused
5 Think on your feet
6 Keep cool, calm and collected
(adapted from Kemp and Nathan, 1989, p. 97)

- *Purpose* — Why are you having the meeting? What are your objectives?
- *Planning and preparation* — Who needs to be at the meeting? What should be on the agenda? When is the best time to hold the meeting? Where and at what time? Who is taking the minutes? (this needs to be organised before the meeting and should not be the chairperson)
- *Content* — Keep the objectives clearly in focus. Plan how to work through the agenda and make best use of time. Consider the contributions from colleagues before moving on to the next item on the agenda.
- *Follow-up* — Circulation of minutes. Was the meeting successful? Implement any agreed action.

Consider using these points in your role as a member of a meeting, as chairperson and in relation to overall evaluation.

Interpersonal skills

Interpersonal skills form the basis of good communication and will enable you to get to know your colleagues, their values, attitudes, personalities, strengths and weaknesses — this is important when you are trying to get the best out of them. It will also enable you to read situations and take appropriate action, and to give thanks, praise and criticism when necessary.

Criticising a colleague may be the most difficult part of your role, particularly when dealing with colleagues who may have more experience than you, are resistant to comment, are dogmatic, or very sensitive, etc. In my experience, face-to-face encounters are crucial in trying to sort out any controversies or difficult situations.

You need to develop a number of different strategies to cope with the varying managerial situations you will encounter. Trying to remain impartial when necessary can be difficult. Keeping details of any discussions along with a record of any disagreement and decision is a healthy sign of good management. It also forms an evidence base for future reference.

SUPPORTING MEETINGS

As a member of the meeting do you:	Always	Sometimes	Never
■ brief yourself as fully as possible beforehand			
■ attend regularly and punctually			
■ participate fully without talking too much			
■ recognise the authority of the chairperson			
■ help to resolve conflicts, rather than generate them			
■ clarify issues rather than confuse them			
■ listen attentively when others are speaking			
■ avoid personal feuds			
■ keep to the point being discussed			
■ avoid over-long and/or anecdotal explanations			
■ appear interested, positive and supportive			
■ ask to chair a meeting			
■ volunteer to take minutes			

CHAIRING MEETINGS

As chairperson of the subject meeting do you:	Always	Sometimes	Never
■ define the purpose			
■ make sure all members can attend			
■ request agenda items and distribute agendas in advance			
■ arrange and organise a suitable venue			
■ have all the necessary papers, information and resources available			
■ conduct the meeting efficiently			
■ control the discussion			
■ encourage individual contributions			
■ balance their contribution with that of others			
■ lead without dictating			
■ deal effectively with problem situations and individuals			
■ ensure the objectives are achieved			
■ make sure everyone knows what is expected of them as a result of a decision made			
■ ensure accurate records are kept			
■ clarify individual follow up action			
■ allow others an opportunity to be chairperson			

EFFECTIVENESS OF MEETINGS

	Yes	No	Sometimes
1 Do the meetings begin on time?			
2 Is there a circulated, democratically constructed agenda?			
3 Is the purpose of meetings clear?			
4 Are meetings minuted?			
5 Are all the items on the agenda relevant or could they have been dealt with by an alternative mode?			
6 Are the meetings and items on the agenda given a designated time or do they carry on regardless?			
7 Is there an opportunity for appropriate teachers to attend and contribute, including part-time staff?			
8 Did the results of the meetings justify the time spent?			
9 Are the minutes given to the Senior Management Team for comment?			
10 Is there a set day and time for meetings?			
11 Could results of meetings have been better?			
12 Are the conclusions of agenda items acted upon?			

© Falmer Press Ltd

Dealing with difficult colleagues

School staffrooms are made up of a variety of colourful personalities and characters, with no two people the same. Coordinating these characters to maintain a whole school approach is one of your great challenges. Inspite of industrious efforts to do this and to establish effective communication and positive relationships, it is inevitable that you will encounter colleagues who are deliberately awkward, difficult to work with, and some you may even feel you dislike.

Difficulties that exist between you and colleagues, or between other members of staff, can lead to negative attitudes, a lack of response and uncooperative behaviour. This can have serious implications for the work you are trying to do. It becomes even more difficult when colleagues know difficulties and tensions exist, but are reluctant to discuss them. In the long term this will inhibit the development of an open, collaborative climate where professional trust is the norm: pretending difficulties do not exist is no solution. *So what do you do?*

Differences of opinion, confrontation and critique are all healthy activities, and are part of community life. It is important to remember that difficulties and differences between people are a product of two or more people. No one person is to blame! Day et al. (1993) remind us that in thinking through ways to improve a relationship, you need to begin by accepting that you have some responsibility in it and for improving it. In short, you could be 50 per cent of the problem!

Everard and Morris (1990) offer a strategy for teachers to consider when faced with conflict. This can be adapted for you to use when working with difficult colleagues:

- Meet face to face and talk as openly as possible about real issues that concern you both.
- State your aims, views and feelings calmly, and avoid repetition.
- Look for common goals, the whole school approach.
- Focus on action rather than events of the past.

- Listen carefully to your colleague's point of view and seek to understand it. You need to show genuine interest.
- Avoid moving onto the attack or defence.
- Try to build on each others' ideas.
- Aim to trust each other and act in good faith.
- Plan clear actions to follow face-to-face discussions.
- Set a date and time to review the issues and progress (if necessary) and keep to it at all costs.

(adapted from Everard and Morris, 1990, p. 102)

Clearly the whole process pivots around your ability to recognise conflict and effectively confront difficult people and difficult situations. You will need to employ your communication skills to solve such difficulties through coalition and negotiation.

Managing change

 The ability to create and manage the future in the way we wish is what differentiates the good manager from the bad manager.

(Harvey-Jones, 1988, p. 96)

Monitoring and evaluation will form a significant part of your role (see also Chapter 3). It will inevitably involve you in the process of change. This could be organised in a formal or informal way and could involve one or several colleagues. Whatever you propose to change consider, 'If you start something it is worth thinking about where it might end'. A systematic approach to change involves planning and decision-making and you will have to take the lead in PE. But, as Harrison (1995) comments, change will never be achieved solely as the result of your plan, government legislation or incidental INSET, 'Change only occurs when teachers believe in the need for it, know where it is going, are committed to it and have some ownership of it' (p. 7). This relates very much to your ability to *manage your colleagues.*

Figure 2.5 outlines a framework for the various stages in the process of change.

FIG 2.5
Stages in the process of change

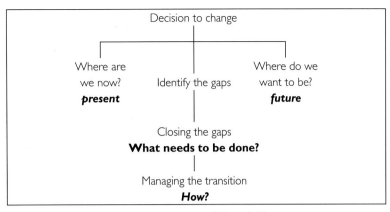

(*Source*: adapted from Everard and Morris, 1990, p. 249)

Conducting an audit of school practice is the first stage in any change process. A curriculum audit will highlight what you are doing well and also signal areas for attention, sometimes known as a 'gap'. Select one area for change and try to plan the process from start to finish. For example: You have identified a lack of summer games, in particular, there is no tennis. Why is this? Try to think laterally particularly when you begin to decide what needs to be done and how. This brings into play all your knowledge about the school, the pupils and your colleagues. It may be simply because there is limited equipment and so perhaps you have to accept this as your responsibility and prioritise tennis equipment as part of you next budget. This may lead to discussions about the value of tennis and how important it is for children to gain some experience: if tennis appears on the curriculum will it 'squeeze' something else out? So, what are your priorities?

Torrington and Weightman (1989) remind us, 'Management is not a box of tricks with a nice drill to suit any eventuality: it is an art that requires clear understanding of issues before the performance can be produced' (p. 11).

The ability to manage the process of change successfully is closely linked to the implementation of the staff and subject development plans outlined in the next chapter.

Chapter 3   Evaluation and development

One of the keys to a successful subject is the quality of the thinking and reflection that takes place. It is important, therefore, that you create time in your busy year to think and evaluate the quality of PE in your school.

An essential and perhaps difficult part of your job will be *evaluating* the PE provision in your school, sometimes referred to as 'quality assurance'. It should be an accepted part of the growth and *development* of the subject. It is not a single, simple activity; it occurs in many forms, for several reasons and can be formal or informal. It is usually a senior management responsibility; however, most headteachers will involve coordinators and expect you to:

- provide a knowledgable overview of the subject's present situation;
- be aware of the strengths and shortcomings in provision of the subject;
- determine likely causes for such shortcomings;
- in conjunction with the head, develop an action plan to correct any shortcomings;
- organise staff development and INSET activities;
- address areas identified by SDPs or OFSTED.

This is reinforced in the 1996 TTA proposals for subject leaders listed on page 39.

- Monitor and evaluate teaching of the subject in the school, taking action as necessary to improve the quality of teaching and learning.
- Monitor and evaluate progress and achievement in the subject by all pupils, including those with special educational needs, taking action as necessary to raise achievement and setting clear targets for improvement, taking account of relevant local and national information.
- Monitor and evaluate the work of all staff involved in teaching the subject at the school and take action as necessary to secure improvement.
- Set expectations for staff and pupils in relation to standards of pupil achievement and the quality of teaching, establishing clear targets for improving and sustaining pupil achievement.
- Monitor, evaluate and review the effects of subject policies, priorities and targets in practice across the school and take the necessary action for improvement.

Many schools are developing policies on subject evaluation. If there is a policy available use it to form the basis of the PE evaluation, so that it fits within the existing system. If your school is still finding its way in terms of evaluation, part of your role, as a middle manager, will involve you in shaping the system and monitoring it so that it works. The following information offers guidance on how to fulfil this role (the principles identified are also reinforced and developed through subsequent Chapters 5 and 8).

Creating a climate for critical reflection

Being critical about and examining your own practice is a normal part of today's climate in education. It is regarded as a natural part of the ongoing need for change and the pursuit of excellence. However, some colleagues, for a variety of reasons, may find evaluation difficult, after all 'I've been doing this for years, why should I change now?' It is not unnatural for some individuals to take negative comments personally and look for someone or something else to blame. So, it is essential that the ethos created is one of support and openness which relates to the need for 'team work' and a whole school approach referred to in Chapter 2. Rigorous reflection also needs to be conducted

Suggestion

Review the current situation
What climate currently exisits in your school?
What evaluation is currently going on?
What do you consider to be the good points?
What would you like to change
How can you help create the right climate?
Are the purposes of evaluation clear?

in a 'business-like' way: if it is carefully planned and objective, it will rise beyond the personal level.

Kemp and Nathan (1989) believe the key to effective evaluation, of your own performance, either as a teacher or a manager, and the performance of the team you manage, is to be open. They suggest this involves:

 openness in accepting and analysing positive criticism having an open mind to suggestions and alternatives opening the process to all people who can make a positive contribution.
(p. 241)

It is easy to argue for this, the challenge is how to put it into practice.

To create a positive climate for change you will need to establish that the main purpose of evaluation is the improvement of children's learning and achievement through a supportive teacher culture. To generate this in PE there are a whole series of questions you will need to collectively address:

- Why evaluate?
- What do we evaluate?
- How will the evaluation be carried out? By whom? When?
- How will the information be used? (action planning)

Why evaluate?

The purpose of evaluation will vary. Davies and Ellison (1994) suggest that evaluation is (or should be) primarily concerned with 'doing things better' (p. 117); it 'uses the past to illuminate the future' (p. 121). Evaluation can be formative or summative. The latter relates to the *accountability* function of evaluation — that is, collecting information to *judge* the quality and assessing achievements. Two examples are OFSTED and end of year school reviews. In contrast to this, the formative (or developmental) approach is seen as a natural part of everyday professional practice involving *critical reflection*. This suggests that information gathered at different times has different purposes. To maximise the use of evaluation data, it is important that information gathered is used both in a developmental and judgmental way leading to overall improvement in practice.

There will be lots of reasons for evaluation and your school policy will identify the more general aims. Aims that are more specific to PE will be your responsibility and should include:

> To determine the staff's effectiveness in delivering physical education.
> To judge the progress and effect of any change you have implemented.
> To evaluate the PE curriculum.
> To evaluate your own performance as coordinator.
> To conduct an audit of resources.
> To evaluate how children with special educational needs are integrated.

The information you gather will provide you with a valuable insight into what is actually going on in PE.

It is important to think about who will be interested in the evaluation, who you have to feedback to and who will have access to any written evaluation report. This could include your colleagues, the governors, the parents, the LEA and/or DfEE. Once you have identified the audience you can identify what they will need to know and what they are likely to do with the information. This will help you decide on your approach and the way in which you will present the report.

What are you evaluating?

Start by identifying the *focus* of the evaluation. In order to make the task more manageable it is wise to limit the focus. The focus could be on the people involved, for example:

- on you and how well you are fulfilling your responsibilities;
- on how well individuals are performing — both teachers and pupils;
- on the whole school team.

Once you have decided the focus you will need to identify the areas to be evaluated. This may be a single element of a person's role or a particular area, for examples:

■ *Extra-curricular programmes* The number of clubs, teams and out-of-school activities can be used as a performance indicator of the quality of the provision.
■ *Subject documentation* This is used as a performance indicator of the quality of planning.
■ *Children's response in lessons* Pupils wearing appropriate kit will give some indication of the school 'ethos' towards appearance and presentation.
■ *Quality of teaching* Use of different teaching styles, differentiation.
■ *Curriculum resource materials* How well is PE provided for.

How do you evaluate?

The emphasis in this section is on making evaluation manageable. Remember, colleagues will be involved in evaluating all the curriculum areas as well as other whole school issues.

You will need to decide, and make clear
■ Who is to carry out the evaluation.
■ When it is to take place.
■ The processes to be used.
■ The specific criteria to be used in making an assessment.

Again, consider what is current practice? What is working? What is not working and how would you like to change it? Will staff evaluate themselves or each other? Many believe that if staff are involved in evaluating their colleagues using an agreed set of criteria there will be a greater commitment to the outcomes than if outsiders evaluate the school using their own criteria (Davies and Ellison, 1994, p. 118). First time around this is not easy as qualified teachers are usually independent in the classroom — having a 'critical friend', a colleague, in to observe you teaching, no matter how confident you feel, can initially be nerve-racking!

'Critical reflection' is not new. Teachers are already engaged in it, as they constantly make judgments about their own performance, the performance of their colleagues and of the whole school. As coordinator, you should build on this and formalise the process, using the 'critical friend' technique to gather information which will assist in designing staff development programmes, subject and school development plans. This will help create an evaluation system that is systematic, flexible and reflective, with a wide evidence base.

Internal evaluation can be a mixture of formal or informal activities providing security for all of those involved. The strategies already in constant use include:

- informal discussions with colleagues;
- formal biannual and annual review meetings;
- observation of classroom practice;
- teacher/pupil surveys;
- teachers' planning;
- displays of work;
- children's assessment.

Many of these strategies are in daily use when assessing children's progress and achievement and can be transferred. Bentley and Watts (1994) provide some useful advice on evaluation through a form of action research — teacher as researcher — which is also promoted by the TTA. This would not only contribute to the school's monitoring and evaluation, but also to staff development and where possible lead to additional qualifications. It is important to note that wherever possible staff development should link with the career plans of you and your colleagues.

Development plans

From any evaluation, internal or external, a picture will emerge of areas that are working well as well as areas that may need development. It is important to report on the strengths that emerge, give praise and credit, as well as gaps in experience, skills or knowledge. Any report that you compile for your colleagues needs to be kept simple and concise so that staff don't feel overwhelmed.

Action planning simply refers to identifying an objective, or objectives, and setting a series of targets and actions, within financial and time frames, in order to meet identified targets.

> ALL EVALUATION MUST FEED INTO A SUBJECT DEVELOPMENT PLAN

> Thomas (1995) advises us that the action plan must be SMART:
> **S**pecific
> **M**easurable
> **A**chievable
> **R**ealistic
> **T**ime constrained (p. 11)

This acronym can help you keep in mind the key elements of a plan. Many teachers find it useful to document the action plan in tabular form and is something that you may find useful. Various examples are illustrated on pages 50 and 51.

> The North Eastern Education and Library Board (NEELB) promote action planning in the form of a 'journey':
> START (where are you now?)
> FINISH (where are you going?)
> TRANSPORT (how will you get there, who will drive, how fast, what route?)
> PASSENGERS (how many involved in the journey, all, a few, will some go ahead, will others follow?)

This process is very similar to managing any process of change which is addressed on pages 36–7.

There are different types of action plans, often referred to as development plans, and it is important that they are seen as interdependent, together they will lead to improved teaching and learning.

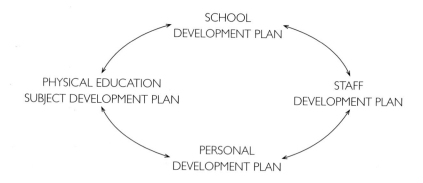

Personal development plans — Evaluating your own performance as a coordinator

Evaluating yourself as a manager is likely to be an ongoing activity as well as part of a summative appraisal, possibly conducted by a deputy head or the headteacher. The expectations on you will relate to the school's job description for subject coordinators and this is a good starting point from which you can compile a list of skills.

In Chapter 2 I outlined leadership as an important part of your role. I suggested good leadership involved personal management, task management and people management. Assessing your performance in personal management will necessitate asking yourself specific questions about how well you managed tasks and colleagues. For example, with task management, are the subject schemes, aims and objectives

- clearly defined in writing?
- readily available?
- derived from the school aims?

Resources .

Is there evidence that the subject areas' resources (facilities, equipment, money, curriculum materials) are

- being used to teach the curriculum effectively?
- of good quality and, where appropriate, in good repair?
- adequately stored with systematic procedures for their use?

People management will involve you in the evaluation of how well your colleagues are working together as a team and how well they are delivering the agreed curriculum. This takes you into the broad area of staff development.

Staff development

Before the 1980s the professional development of teachers was an ad hoc affair with little coherent planning. By the late 1980s INSET became a familiar term for all teachers. This was superseded in the 1990s by Continuing Professional Development (CPD) as a model for staff development, which has benefited from changes in funding, an expansion of providers, venues and methods, and an understanding that CPD is an entitlement for all teachers.

Education is constantly changing: new initiatives; short timescales for implementation, and ever-increasing accountability means that primary schools need well-informed and highly motivated teachers. As Jones et al. (1989) commented 'The Status Quo is not an option' (p. 4) change is an ongoing process. Professional development for teachers is an essential part of any strategy designed to meet the changing needs of education. This, coupled with the fact that many teachers will have limited experience and training, means that we must expect that teachers will need support and assistance.

Do you know who is responsible for overall staff development in your school? Of course, the answer will depend on how your school is run and your role as subject coordinator. Undoubtedly subject specific development will be the responsibility of individual subject coordinators, but during my interviews with PE coordinators it became apparent that staff development in physical education is variable and can be a rare event. One coordinator reported that in her school over a period of six years she had been on one course, when she was first appointed as coordinator, but the whole staff had had just two sessions; a half day on games and one day on dance. Finding time to work with staff can be very difficult, particularly if PE is low down the list of the school's priorities, but this is all the more reason why you should try to gain more time and ensure that whatever time is available is put to good use.

Any programme must be efficient and effective if professional development is to occur. Teachers will expect you to guide and lead them in areas of subject development. This is a challenge to all teachers acting as coordinators. NQTs and newly appointed PE co-ordinators, in particular, would be wise to gain some experience of working with colleagues and getting to know the way the school works before assuming too much responsibility for staff development programmes. It should be seen as a medium- to long-term aim, giving you the opportunity to get to know colleagues, to seek advice and build on previous practice. The first question is: What do I have to do?

Check your responsibility as PE coordinator and confirm with the headteacher the contribution you will be expected to make to the school staff development programme. At the same time try to gain his/her support for the inclusion of physical education in the school and staff development plans. Confirm the budget that you will have to support your work in this area.

Once you have found out your commitments you can begin to work on your contribution to the overall programme. LEA advisers, HEIs, local or regional cluster groups and your friendly neighbourhood school are all sources of help, inspiration and advice.

Managing staff development

This section offers practical guidance on how to set up and implement a successful staff development (SD) programme, or specific INSET course.

It is important to remember that many teachers will have experienced 30 hours or less initial teacher training in PE, and perhaps your own training may mean that you too have limited expertise. More than ever before — with The National Curriculum, changes in health and safety, increased cases of litigation against teachers and schools — a well-organised staff development programme for physical education is a necessity. You will need to provide practical assistance with teaching and learning, as well as background subject knowledge. With so many activity areas in PE, the latter might be based around any concerns colleagues have with the activities (athletics, dance, gymnastics, games, outdoor and adventurous activities and swimming) they have agreed to cover. This was identified by OFSTED (1995) who expressed the need for more INSET as a key issue for primary schools in order to give teachers the confidence to teach the full National Curriculum in PE at Key Stages 1 and 2. But it is not only your colleagues that you need to support: remember, it is also important that you look after your own development and take time to seek assistance to help develop your own practice.

Managing a staff development programme is an integral part of your monitoring and evaluation role and will involve you in various activities and sequential processes. You will need to:

- review the current situation and help set a suitable climate for improving PE: get to know staff, encourage openness and sharing, develop trust, try to get colleagues to accept you for what you are (an interested colleague who is there to help);
- work within the school staff development policy;
- identify specific needs: these should arise out of individual staff concerns, be appropriate to the varying needs of the whole staff, reflect teachers' values and be agreed collectively for the subject and relate to external considerations;
- plan the programme (short, medium and long term) including an estimation of costs;
- monitor and evaluate teaching and learning.

You may feel that you need to receive some INSET training to help you fulfil these duties, but this is unlikely, and you will largely depend on your existing organisation and leadership skills, your ability to negotiate with colleagues and other agencies, and your counselling skills.

There is no one model for staff development but what is common is the need to ensure that the model adopted is suitable to the staff involved. If teachers are to be committed to change and participate meaningfully in the process then any staff development must address areas identified by teachers as beneficial. A well-organised programme of development should motivate and stimulate teachers and pay dividends for pupils and the school. A long-term goal is for teachers to drive their own development programme that meets their own personal desires and ambitions.

Self-evaluation for colleagues

The first stage in creating a climate for change is to encourage and promote self-evaluation: there can be no real staff development unless individual teachers continually monitor and improve their individual practice (individual staff development). That is, teachers should be encouraged to follow a model of *reflective practice*: being active in their own development while remaining aware of external developments and pressures. It is this first stage that is often most difficult to implement, but it lays the foundations for all future work. It can be conducted on an informal basis or in a more structured and formal way, and will form the basis of identifying an individual's needs. It is important that the self-evaluation exercise offers an opportunity for teachers to identify:

■ what they are already doing well — their strengths;
■ what is not working — their weaknesses and concerns;
■ any need for change;
■ staff development needs.

At the end of any self-evaluation process an action plan needs to be developed, see pp. 50–1.

Whole school evaluation

The next stage involves all teachers and is about whole school approach to improvement. This can involve different approaches, but wherever possible should come from the teachers. Pollard and Tanen (1987) suggest starting from issues raised by individual staff that have whole school implications. Another approach, presented by Easen (1985) focuses on a mutual sharing of issues and concerns and agreeing on an agenda for development.

In addition to internal self-evaluation, schools and teachers need to become more comfortable with external evaluation. OFSTED, albeit sometimes a stressful process, can be very useful in highlighting issues for staff and school development that may otherwise be overlooked.

It is also important for you to keep up to date with what is happening in the world of physical education. Are there any new initiatives which need to be considered and implemented?

Designing the staff development programme

There are various methods available, but designing their own programme can be an important part of the process if teachers are to take ownership and put the programme into practice. Questionnaires can be used to provide a very broad overview of teacher needs and will encourage them to think generally about their teaching and any areas of concern. For example, the staff audit below is used at Cranfield School: a summary of the answers is used to plan curriculum support. This method involves you in 'interactive' management with colleagues and should help promote sharing and team work as suggested in Chapter 2.

Staffing Audit — Individual Response
Strengths:
- teaching skills in games and gymnastics
- good use of different teaching styles

Concerns:
- teaching tactics and rules of the different games
- keeping 30+ children safe in a hall for 45 minutes every Tuesday
- recording assessment

Needs:
- progression and continuity ideas for Key Stage 2 apparatus work in gymnastics

Alternatively you could focus on what Moyles (1988) considers the basic characteristics of the effective teacher. She outlines six categories which can be illustrated on a proforma and used to audit staff strengths, concerns and needs as indicated below. The information collected should form the basis for INSET provision.

Staffing audit	Strengths	Concerns	Needs
Curriculum content			
Relationships with children			
Children's progress and achievement			
Discipline and child management			
Classroom organisation and display			
Teachers' professional attitude/personality			

Or, you could use the OFSTED criteria, outlined on p. 119, or the existing school appraisal system. By using such formats it should make the data more relevant to a number of accountability exercises. It would seem appropriate for the school to adopt an agreed format so as to generate some consistency and cohesion of approach. The exercise is intended to be quick with teachers making immediate responses and not thinking too deeply. Honesty is important. Here two examples of staff development plans.

Physical Education Staff Development Action Plan — Inset Needs

	SHORT TERM	MEDIUM TERM	LONG TERM
INTENTIONS			
WHAT is to be done?			
HOW will it be done?			
WHEN and WHERE will it be done?			
WHO will be involved? and in what way?			
RESOURCE IMPLICATIONS			
Financial			
Time			
Equipment			
Accommodation			

AVONDALE Staff Development Action Plan
Prepared by .... Date ....

YEAR	AIMS	ISSUE	OUTCOME	WHO	WHEN	COST
YEAR 1						
YEAR 2						
YEAR 3						

Organising INSET

When planning for staff development you can use a variety of sources of information and activities. The freedom of schools to organise their own INSET provision also enables schools to buy-in the expertise of local specialists to come into the school and work alongside staff. Make use of any links with local teacher trainers and local authority advisers or consultants to offer curriculum support and provide details of various local and regional courses.

Model your own good practice, and that of others in the school, to help colleagues gain new ideas and encourage a sharing of information. This can be done through demonstration materials, providing displays of children's work or by making use of video recordings. This type of support activity was endorsed by HMI in 1991 who reported that notes written by coordinators which included advice on lesson planning, the presentation of movement tasks, observation and discussion, criteria for achieving good quality movements and progression, management of materials and class control were considered to be particularly helpful for colleagues.

You may find the following list of activities suitable for staff development, once you have identified which activities are best suited to meeting your needs as identified in your plan. When running any INSET sessions. You will also need to consider: time available; resources and funding; balance and range of activities. Remember, not all SD needs extra money and additional resources: joint activities, working in partnership with other schools, asking advisors, can all help to maximise opportunities and makes good use of resources.

Staff development activities may include:
- full staff subject review
- curriculum planning
- individual research
- observation of good practice
- teacher appraisal
- producing documentation
- watching videos
- joining working parties, either school based, with outside agencies or with local schools
- job exchanges
- demonstrations from pupils (own/colleagues), lesson cameos, you teach staff
- demonstrations with teachers as pupils
- demonstrations where staff teach staff or invited guest tutor

- examination of exemplar material
- workshops led by staff and or coaches/consultants/support agencies
- discussion of documents/publications led by staff and or consultants/coaches

Ways of working may include:
- working in groups, either task based, open discussion, brainstorming
- whole group work, question and answer, plenary
- individual work aide memoir, self-reflection and evaluation, checklists
- attending courses, local, regional, national; short or long; school based or residential; part day or whole day; twilight or before school; modular accredited or certificated; specialist or general; cross-phase or cross-curricular; practical or theoretical.

The key to successful INSET is to use the appropriate method for different activities and purposes.

Preparing the INSET session

Thorough preparation and purpose are essential when organising the staff development day in PE. Ensure that you:
- clarify the purpose of the day;
- collect the resources;
- confirm the accommodation;
- think about and prepare the detail of the programme: structure of the day; activities; preparation of handouts, worksheets, etc.

Running the INSET session is very similar to running your own classes for the day, except your pupils are bigger! Be sure to be in early to set up equipment and activities. Try to delegate different responsibilities so that you are left to 'oversee' and monitor rather that be tied up with details. Try to predict some potential problems e.g. OHP's paperwork, resources and numbers changing etc. so that you are not thrown on the day.

Systematic follow-up is important if INSET is not to be seen as divorced from day-to-day activities of teachers. You might like to encourage some of the follow-up activities:

- report back sessions;
- display of any materials, resources resulting from the INSET;
- written reports, circulated to staff, parents and governors as appropriate.

Evaluating staff development

All staff development should, as a means of good practice, be monitored and evaluated. It should be an integral and ongoing part of the programme. In 1986 the Government defined the purpose of evaluating INSET as related to how far it has contributed to more effective and efficient delivery of the education service. Headteachers will want to know whether the programme is giving value for money and you too will want to know if it has been of value to the staff and ultimately will benefit the pupils.

Teachers will naturally talk about their INSET experiences, albeit briefly on occasions, the job of the coordinator is to extract these comments via verbal feedback or a short questionnaire and try and put them into some meaningful evaluation summary. This information in turn will help work towards improvement.

External evaluations are usually formal evaluations and are carried out by local advisers, consultants or OFSTED inspectors. In these types of evaluation, the criteria is clearly defined, information is collected, and conclusions are documented in some form of official report. This form of evaluation usually happens in cycles (for example, every five years) so there is a greater need to focus on your own internal self-evaluation. However, it is worth taking note of what these external evaluations will look at and link this with your own subject approach.

Your work on monitoring and evaluating PE will form a valuable foundation for any external inspection, consequently

Suggestion

How might the staff development day be monitored and evaluated?
In the light of this chapter, review and assess your own staff development plan for PE. If there isn't one, then now is the time to get the ball rolling. You could ask another PE coordinator to evaluate your plan and act as a 'critical friend'.

the outcome will give you some clear indication of how well you are doing your job. I like Cross and Byrnes' (1995) idea that inspectors will be looking for:

> ❝ *thinking coordinators . . . who are engaged with the task of improving standards in the school.* (p. 80)

A formal inspection can only establish a picture of what is going on during a particular week in the life of a school. But through examining documentation, talking to teachers and pupils, looking at displays, facilities and the organisation of equipment stores the inspector will learn a great deal about how the subject is managed. The inspection framework (OFSTED, 1995) specifically identifies the following areas for comment:

- Educational standards achieved by pupils at the school
    Attainment and progress
    Attitudes, behaviour and personal development
    Attendance
- Quality of education provided
    Teaching
    The curriculum and assessment
    Pupils' spiritual, moral, social and cultural development
    Support, guidance and pupils' welfare Partnership with
    parents and the community
- The Management and efficiency of the school
- Leadership and Management
- Staffing, accommodation and learning resources
- The efficiency of the school

Become familiar with the up-to-date inspection framework as this will clearly outline the areas to be inspected, and wherever possible align your own school-based approach to subject evaluation with the OFSTED framework. For example, any subject review should prioritise areas requiring attention identifying short- and long-term action.

At the end of an OFSTED inspection you will receive an oral summary followed by a written report some six weeks later. If there are any areas related to PE then these will have to be linked to any existing action plan or form the basis of a new plan. A good thinking coordinator should, in my view, be able to virtually write their own inspection report and identify strength and weaknesses. To do so at the end of each year as a form of review is good practice and forms the basis for next year's agenda. This in turn sets a good standard for others to see.

Partnerships with Initial Teacher Education (ITE)

In recent years there has been a significant shift towards school-based training and teachers' involvement as mentors. It is very likely that you will be involved in this process, at a school and personal level. You may not act as a mentor yourself, but you may have colleagues who will. So what does it involve and how can you set about implementing the programme? I have been involved in ITE for a long time and it is very important that you engage in the right programme.

Context of ITE partnership

Since Circulars 9/92 and 14/93, schools have assumed greater responsibility for training activities, but why should your school get involved? Working with student teachers can offer a great deal of satisfaction, seeing them develop into teachers. It can also be used to motivate staff and be used as a means of professional development for them:

- it encourages the sharing of new ideas;
- the process of analysing one's own practice as a model for student teachers should have a positive effect on one's own teaching.

Different types of partnerships

Universities and colleges run various schemes, no two are the same and this makes it quite complicated if you work with a number of different institutions. You may also get involved with SCITT or the Articled Teachers approach. Whatever you do it must be acceptable to the staff and school. Working in partnership is not easy so there must be good communication and an agreed approach. When offering mentoring in PE it is useful if you make contact with the PE lecturers and establish positive links.

Role of the mentor

When writing about *What is Mentoring?* Taylor and Stephenson (1996) analysed various definitions and concluded

> *Since the world is blurred and fuzzy and there are no nice clear cut definitions but only degrees of resemblance and dissimilarity, then there are no nice handy clear cut prescriptions about mentoring.* (p. 35)

One working description of mentoring is the general activity of supporting and advising students undertaken by a teacher who has undergone a course of training to support the learning of student teachers in school. Mentors have a vital role to play in the induction, supervision and assessment of school-based work (Primary *PGCE handbook*, 1995/96, p. 115), but it's not quite as simple as this. Stephenson and Taylor (1996) examine three levels at which mentoring can be examined:

> *. . . as a principle or idea or concept . . . vague ideas in the minds of the gods*
> *. . . as a programme from a perspective of those that set-up the mentoring schemes*
> *. . . [as] the interaction between mentors and protégé* (p. 25)

It is clear from the literature that 'mentor' and 'mentoring' are open to various interpretations in different applications and settings (Williams, 1996; Mawer, 1996). This leaves the teacher to some extent as an autonomous professional, doing the best they can in their own partnership context. What will be clear are the partnership arrangements that outline details of the roles and responsibilities and which must serve as a guide to 'what do I have to do if I am a mentor?' Class teachers will need guidance on this if they are mentoring in PE.

The University of Exeter Partnership Scheme is unique to the institution and its location. The school based mentor's roles and responsibilities are described as:

Each partner school has a Designated Mentor who manages the school's involvement with Initial Teacher Education, oversees communication with the University and monitors the quality of school provision. The Mentor is responsible for identifying, managing and advising all other school-based personnel designated to work with student-teachers. It is the responsibility of the Mentor to ensure that a programme of induction into the whole school is provided and that student-teachers have the appropriate documentation on the school's policies and practice. The Mentor is responsible for the student-teacher throughout the placement, including monitoring files and overseeing the completion of School Directed Activities. It is also the responsibility of the Mentor to ensure that all assessment documentation is completed. In some larger primary schools there may be additional Mentors who assist the Designated Mentor. More detailed information is also made available regarding the role of the Class Teacher as a craft specialist.

Similary, the Open University PGCE designated mentor has the following responsibilities during the student's school experience:

- to support the student in developing subject knowledge and application, and classroom teaching skills
- to carry out observations and offer regular feedback designed to help students identify strengths and weaknesses in line with the policy laid down for the PGCE
- to assess competences and professional qualities, and to support the student in developing evidence for the professional development portfolio
- to hold weekly mentor sessions with the student teacher to review progress and the action plan for future development
- to provide a School Report at the end of each school placement, providing information on student progress, school-based time completed, and in School Report Stage 3 competences achieved
- to support the student in carrying out course requirements during school experiences, for example discussing school policies, arranging interviews with key personnel, facilitating the collection of data
- to provide the student support in personal matters, and to liaise with the course tutor at the joint meeting held at each stage of the course
- to liaise with the school coordinator about the school experience programme for each stage and student progress on the course.

(The Open University, 1996, pp. 9–10)

Getting involved in ITE can be a very demanding yet rewarding experience. Whenever students are involved in delivering PE in your school it will be up to you to ensure that they receive appropriate support. You should also make use of them as a resource, perhaps offering you some new insight or ideas into current practice in PE.

Part two

What the PE coordinator needs to know

Chapter 4
What you need to know
about PE

Chapter 5
Effective teaching and learning
in PE

Chapter 6
Developing a framework for
safe practice

What you need to know about PE

Understanding physical education, and in particular good practice, involves looking at both the subject and the research that outlines the qualities of effective physical education teachers. Definitions will vary according to the school and community requirements, as well as those agreed by national organizations such as The British Association of Advisers and Lecturers in Physical Education (BAALPE), The Physical Education Association United Kingdom (PEAUK) and OFSTED.

This chapter will firstly focus on physical education as a foundation subject and outline reasons why it has its place in the school curriculum. This will help you increase your own subject knowledge and gain familiarity with the National Curriculum definition of PE and the statutory Programmes of Study (PoS).

To summarise, physical education:
- is a foundation subject in the National Curriculum. Teachers are considered skilled experts responsible for delivering the programmes of study.
- forms part of the whole school curriculum. It is a whole school responsibility, shared by all teachers, for all pupils.
- contributes to extra curricular provision. Provided by teachers, qualified coaches and parents for all pupils.
- provides a basis for sport and links with the community. Some pupils extend their involvement in sport and join outside clubs.

PE as a foundation subject — a rationale

As a coordinator you will already know what PE can offer young children and why it should be part of the curriculum. The challenge is to convince your governors, parents, senior staff and colleagues of its benefits so that they too are committed to the subject and understand the need for time and resources to be allocated. They should look to you for guidance and be prepared to listen to what you have to say about the aims of PE. Once they have a clear understanding of these aims you can begin to promote the serious educational benefits of the subject and hopefully dispel the idea of it being play — a time for a change from classroom lessons.

There are numerous descriptions of the *aims* of PE. In their non-statutory guidance for PE, the National Curriculum Council (NCC) presented a set of aims which outlined its contribution to the overall education of young people. They claimed that through engagement in purposeful physical activity pupils could lead full and valuable lives. More specifically physical education can

develop physical competence and help to promote physical development;

teach pupils through experience, to know about and value the benefits of participation in physical activity whilst at school and throughout life;

develop appreciation of skilful and creative performances across the areas of activity.　　　　　　　　　　(NCC, 1992, p. 5)

Additionally, physical education contributes to

the development of personal problem-solving skills;

the establishment of self-esteem through the development of physical confidence;

the development of interpersonal skills.　　　　　　　(p. 5)

Concluding,

❝ *Physical activity combines with the thinking involved in making decisions and selecting, refining, judging, and adapting movements. Through these activities pupils should be encouraged to develop personal qualities of commitment, fairness and enthusiasm.* (adapted from p. 5)

The potential of PE is similarly promoted by Sanderson (1994)

❝ *PE experiences make valuable contributions to the development of the whole child by offering integrated physical, motor skill, cognitive, personal and social, creative and aesthetic education.* (p. 55)

Aims are general expressions of intent (Cohen and Manion, 1989, p. 29), and different people will define aims using different language with different emphases. Understanding this diversity of aims is the first stage in planning (see also Part Three of this book): **thinking about and expressing what you want pupils to learn in PE will be one of your most important policy statements**.

The following general headings outline the broad aims of PE:

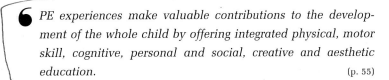

- ■ Physical development and motor skill development;
- ■ Health education;
- ■ Safety education;
- ■ Spiritual, moral, social and cultural development;
- ■ Cognitive development;
- ■ Creative and Aesthetic education.

Physical activity — physical and motor skill development

Early years children and children of primary school age seem to have an natural interest and enthusiasm for activity. They usually have a natural aptitude to 'play' and it is the subtle structuring of this play that provides PE with the opportunity to lay the foundations of physical skills in preparation for lifelong participation. However, it is this emphasis on the physical side that often inhibits teachers who feel less confident with their own ability. Williams (1989) identifies the paradox that teachers face:

> ❝ . . . it is the physical nature of the subject which gives it its distinct identity and its unique place in the curriculum, it is this very physical nature which places it at the periphery of the subject.
>
> (p. 19)

This also emerged during an interview with a coordinator who felt

> ❝ [many of] my colleagues feel intimidated because they are not very good at doing the activities they have to get the children to do. Some certainly don't like getting hot and sweaty. Others, who are quite able, have a totally different attitude once they change into their tracksuits, most of the time anyway, and get stuck in.

PE focuses on the body, on physical experiences and the acquisition of physical skills. Arnold (1979) proposed three dimensions in which movement, physical activity, can be an educational medium. These can be summarised as:

■ education in movement — involving experience of activity;
■ education through movement — using activity to achieve aims which are not necessarily intrinsic to the movement; and
■ education about movement — developing understanding about concepts.

The types of physical activity available are themselves diverse and can be defined in various ways. Most recently, the statutory National Curriculum defined six activity areas (according to the nature of the activity): athletic activities, dance, games (invasion, net/wall, striking and fielding), gymnastics activities, outdoor and adventurous activities, and swimming. These might change as the curriculum is revised and developed, but they are now commonly recognised as the key areas of experience forming the essential programmes of study for physical education. Through these different programmes of physical activity it is intended that pupils should experience and receive:

> ❝ . . . a broad and balanced vigorous exercise involving various muscle groups; different types of exercise to develop control

*and coordination, flexibility, strength, suppleness: and overall
skill development.*   (DES, 1991, p. 28)

Specifically, throwing and catching in games, balancing and
travelling in dance and gymnastics, jumping and running,
diving in swimming, and so on.

Health education

This is considered an important part of PE, which promotes
physical health, and the social and mental well-being of
pupils. Aspects of health education in PE feature as part of the
general requirements of the 1995 National Curriculum Orders
and apply across all Key Stages. These can be summarised as:

■ the importance of physical activity and healthy lifestyles;
  experiencing different physical activities; learning about
  posture and how to use the body, how the body works, the
  changes that occur to the body during exercise, the effects
  of exercise on the body and personal hygiene;

■ the promotion of positive attitudes, observing rules and
  regulations, relating to performance; working with others
  and working alone; coping with success and limitations;
  consolidating performance;

■ aspects of safety; being aware of self discipline and the
  need to follow codes of behaviour in various situations; safe
  dress; using equipment; need to warm up and cool down.
  (DFE, 1995)

conclusion

Health education is identified as a cross-curricular theme
which should pervade the whole school curriculum (DES,
1991) This is discussed further in Part Three.

Safety education

Safety education can complement and develop the focus on
health. PE is recognised in Croner's legal guide (1987) as a
high risk subject that involves children in activities which by
their very nature can be potentially challenging and hazardous.
Although it is the teacher's responsibility to ensure a safe
learning environment (see Chapter 6), they also have to
develop children's awareness of safety and teach them to

become responsible for their own safety and that of others (DES, 1991, p. 65).

An important aspect of safety is how we use, and possibly abuse, the body. Through PE children can learn about posture, appropriate forms of exercise which may help promote good health. PE also involves using various equipment. The safe handling, storage and use of this equipment is central to our overall programme aims.

Another form of safety is developing children's attitudes towards the different rules, laws, codes of play and forms of etiquette in various activities. Children need to understand the reasons for adhering to such regulations.

Spiritual, moral, social and cultural development

Through PE, pupils can be offered experiences to increase their knowledge, develop a positive self-image and self-esteem and promote their understanding of the values and beliefs which promotes their spiritual awareness and self-knowledge. Through activities that involve group work and conformity to rules and regulations, children also begin to learn right from wrong and, with support, nursery pupils can become aware of what is acceptable or unacceptable behaviour. Older pupils should learn to make moral decisions through the application of reason, even though they may not cope quite so securely with problems in which they are emotionally involved; their learning about moral issues may be at a different point to their behaviour values. Through these opportunities, children will learn to accept group rules, to relate to others, to take responsibility for their own actions (self-discipline), and demonstrate initiative. Through links with external agencies, they will be able to participate in the community, understand about citizenship, and learn about their own cultural traditions and the diversity of others (OFSTED, 1995, p. 82).

Cognitive development

Many people think PE is about playing and doing things which involve limited thinking skills. But one only needs to consider what happens in a variety of PE situations to appreciate the level of thinking involved. For example, a child is standing holding a ball and has to pass it to someone else in the team. First the child has to think about *who* she or he is going to pass to, then the *type* of pass, overarm, underarm, bounce, etc. In dance, for example, putting two movements together involves thinking about which movement should be first, should both movements be fast or slow or one fast and one slow, and so on — the examples are endless. PE therefore provides experiences where pupils engage in decision-making, problem-solving, planning, adapting, creating, selecting and judging. Very often children can also be involved in evaluation and self-assessment. Not only do these activities contribute to children's cognitive development but also to the development of personal transferable skills which should serve them well in all aspects of their life.

Creative and aesthetic education

PE offers children opportunities to be involved in linking actions and creating sequences of movements, their own and that of others, in a variety of contexts. Learning to appreciate qualities of movement is an important aspect of aesthetic education and PE offers children opportunities to develop 'feelings' about movement which can trigger their imaginations and generate different forms of expression. With guidance children can apply these feelings, moods and ideas to other aspects of their life and begin to learn to share these with others.

Every school will need to decide on a set of general aims which are articulated through the school policy and curriculum statements for PE. The learning opportunities that teachers create, via different teaching styles and patterns of organisation and pupil grouping (see Chapter 5) will all contribute to achieving these aims. Examples of practice are illustrated in Part Three.

PE is more than just doing

In the past assessment in PE has traditionally been associated with *performance*. Typical schemes of work would have identified a selection of *physical skills* to be taught, mastered and measured. However, through reading and interpreting both the 1992 and the revised 1995 Orders you will probably have noted that PE has been broadened to:

> ❝ . . . *involve pupils in the continuous processes of planning, performing and evaluating. This applies to all areas of activity.*
>
> (1995, p. 2)

This is also explicitly evident in the End of Key Stage programme statements and descriptors. Clay (1995) offers some guidance on what these areas mean:

Performing — Look for appropriate solutions to tasks and the ways in which children find solutions to physical problems. As children move throughout the Key Stage you need to look at the ways in which children perform in each area of activity and consider the extent of their increased competence and versatility. Children should begin to adapt and refine their actions to suit changing circumstances. Other aspects of their performance include their mastery of dynamic qualities, their use of space and their understanding of safety principles.

Planning — You need to consider the way in which children plan before or during performance, the decisions they make in envisioning or anticipating actions, the understanding they display and the effect of their planning on subsequent performance. As children move through the Key Stage good planning involves:

> thinking ahead
> anticipating responses of others
> working cooperatively
> working in pairs and small groups.

Evaluating — At Key Stage 1 children should be capable of making simple judgements about their own and others' performance and by Key Stage 2 they should be able to observe more accurately. Teachers should take account of the ways in which children evaluate during performance, their skills in observing and comparing and the use they make of evaluations.

(p. 3)

Having recognised that PE can contribute to all of these three interrelated areas it is important to note that the revised 1995 Orders places the emphasis on performance to give greater weight to the practical nature of the subject (Gilliver, 1995), and therefore focusing on the physical development of children. From personal experience I would have to agree with this,

Suggestion

Review your current PE rationale. What are your aims? Do you cover the six broad areas mentioned on p. 65? Do you provide opportunities for performing, planning and evaluating?

as it is the practical and physical achievement that signifies the uniqueness of the subject. That said, however, practical performance cannot be divorced from the cognitive, planning and evaluating aspects if it is to be a holistic experience.

Physical education is about the education of the whole individual, and involvement with others. Its uniqueness is the physical component. As coordinator, one of your most important jobs will be to guide and convince colleagues about the aims of physical education, beyond those of letting off steam and a rest from other lessons. The aims that your school endorses need to form the basis of your school policy statement for physical education. (Developing such a statement is developed further in Part 3.) Once the aims have been agreed you can begin to make decisions, involving your colleagues, about the content of the PE curriculum. Examples of how these aims might feature in a school policy are presented in Part 3.

The National Curriculum provides a framework of legal requirements that outline what each school curriculum must provide:

- the Programmes of Study as laid out in the general requirements and each key stage;
- a broad and balanced experience;
- entitlement experiences for all through equal access and opportunity.

The National Curriculum includes a number of general requirements and the six statutory activity areas, distributed across the primary phase. The different areas are intended to form the basis of a broad and balanced experience. This recognises that not all children enjoy the same activities and not all children will be motivated to meet their potential if the curriculum is too narrow. It is important, therefore, that teachers aim to promote the benefits of all activity areas and not favour some to the detriment of others, so you may need to outline the specific value and benefits of each activity to pupils, teachers, headteachers and governors. The Programmes of Study set out what pupils should be taught:

> **general requirements** apply to all Key Stages and should be taught through all the areas of activity;

common requirements must be taught through all the areas of activity for the Key Stage to meet the objectives set out in the end of key stage descriptions;

activity areas (activity specific) refer to each area of activity at each Key Stage (athletics, dance, games, gymnastic activities, outdoor and adventurous activities and swimming).

Activity areas

Athletic activities

Running, jumping and throwing are three athletic skills that can be used in any school playground. They are core skills which all children should develop. These serve not only as foundation skills for participation in many other activities (games — running with the ball and throwing to a team mate; gymnastics — jumping onto and off a box) but they also contribute to all-round physical development, promoting muscular strength, stamina, speed, endurance, flexibility and cardiovascular health.

Athletics is well known for organised events, competitions, and the measurement of achievement. This provides opportunities for children to work with various equipment and cope with open rivalry in a healthy and positive way. Sports days, mini-Olympics and inter-form or -house competitions are school events which enrich the curriculum and offer exciting opportunities to develop cross-curricular themes.

Athletic activities feature as specific programmes of study for pupils at Key Stages 2, 3, 4. This formal developmental structure is designed to give children early experiences of performance and control, which lead on to more specialist track and field events. Whilst it does not feature as a statutory requirement for Key Stage 1, it could still feature on your curriculum through games activities; for example, running and throwing are essential foundation skills in all invasion games.

Dance

Dance, compulsory at Key Stages 1 and 2, specifically contributes to developing children's forms of expression and communication, their use of imagination and non-verbal communication, and the ability to explore and compose their ideas and feelings through movement. In addition, dance promotes technical and performance skills focusing, at Key Stage 1, on the basic actions of travelling, jumping, turning, gesture, transference of weight, and stillness. These are used to develop pupils' body control, sense of rhythm, coordination, balance, poise and elevation. The performance of movement patterns and phrases, using contrasts in dynamics (speed, shape, tension and continuity) and space (direction, levels), helps children to learn how to structure dances. Dancing individually and with other children helps them to understand how their movement in space has implications for others. Looking at dances, observing each other, videos and productions, some of which may be traditional, encourages them to describe and interpret what they see.

These basic actions form a foundation for Key Stage 2 which is designed to build on early experiences and improve pupils' control through developing the varying dynamics and spatial patterns of movement. Pupils should engage in composition, creating and structuring dances, with a clear start, middle and end. They should learn to express feelings and moods through movement using simple characters and narratives, to respond to various stimuli, including music. They should experience dance from a variety of cultural contexts (for example, South Asian) and periods in time (for example, Rock 'n' Roll). The ability to view dance with increasing awareness of content, structure, meaning and style should be developed as the pupils describe, analyse, interpret and evaluate their own and other dance works.

Gymnastics

Very much like dance, gymnastics activities focus on body management. At Key Stage 1 the focus is on the basic actions of travelling using hands and feet, turning, rolling, jumping, balancing, swinging and climbing. These individual movements can be developed into short sequences and be performed on both the floor and appropriate apparatus. This involves pupils working with different equipment, learning how to safely lift, carry, place and use apparatus. This work progresses into Key Stage 2, where children develop and refine these basic skills; are introduced to different ways of rolling, turning, swinging, jumping, climbing, balancing and travelling on hands and feet; learn how to adapt these on the floor and apparatus; think about changes of shape, speed and directions; and develop longer, more complex sequences of actions, on floor and apparatus.

Apparatus work for pupils is one of the exciting parts of gymnastics and provides a variety of challenging experiences. School gymnasia differ in the type apparatus they have but it usually relates to flat surfaces such as benches, beams, boxes and tables, climbing frames and ladders, ropes and sometimes bars for swinging. See pages 131–3 for further information.

Games

Games emerged in the revised National Curriculum as the only compulsory Programme of Study throughout all Key Stages. The main principle is that children should develop a balance of skills across a range of games activities which have some common principles of play. The games activities have thus been sub-divided into three main categories:

Invasion	Net/Wall	Striking/Fielding
basketball	badminton	baseball
football	fives	cricket
handball	squash	rounders
hockey	table-tennis	softball
lacrosse	tennis	stoolball
netball	volleyball	
rugby		

In the early years the emphasis is on simplified versions of recognised team and individual games. The Key Stage 1 programme aims to develop foundation skills, gradually adapting and refining these through Key Stage 2 into mini forms of adult games; for example, hockey at primary school would focus on uni-hoc and 5, 6 or 7 aside, rugby would focus on 'tag' and tennis on short tennis. Some more able children may be developing more specialised skills playing at a competitive level; several National Governing Bodies hold regional and national competitions for the under 11s. Children should be taught to play individually, in pairs and in small groups through both cooperative and competitive situations. This involves simplified versions of games such as 1 v 1, 2 v 1, 3 v 3, 5 v 5 and 7 v 7.

The content of the games teaching, throughout Key Stages 1 and 2, revolves around children learning common elements of playing games, including:

1 **Core skills** These are identified as essential prerequisites to the playing of games and as pupils progress through the Key Stages the emphasis moves from general techniques to more specific techniques involving specialist equipment:
   - *sending skills*: passing striking, kicking, bowling and rolling;
   - *receiving skills*: stopping, trapping, gathering, catching;
   - *travelling skills*: running with and without a ball, whilst carrying or dribbling a ball, chasing, dodging.
   All of these require decisions about speed, space, height, distance, positioning and shielding.
2 **Principles of play — tactics and strategies** for example, in short tennis pupils need to know where to stand when receiving a serve, what to do when trying to 'attack' a poor ground-stroke, or how to try and move your opponent around the court, and so on.
3 **Rules, scoring systems and officiating** throughout the development of games knowledge and understanding, pupils must have opportunities to observe performance, understand the etiquette and rules of the various games.
4 **Games making** Delivery of games material should also involve pupils in composing and planning their own practices, make-up and refine their own games.
   Safety awareness for individual safety as well as the safety of others should permeate all learning.

Providing pupils with a balanced games education should develop pupils' personal competence and understanding thus facilitating more effective and enjoyable participation not only as players but as knowledgeable spectators in later life. In order to provide these experiences teachers, many of whom have taught using traditionally didactic teaching styles, where the emphasis has been on technical skill development and teacher control, will need to develop a whole range of teaching styles and imaginative methods of task organization, particularly at Key Stage 2. This is addressed in further detail in the next chapter.

Outdoor and adventurous activities (OAA)

Outdoor and Adventurous Activities are intended to develop the skills necessary to meet challenges of a physical nature, problem-solving, using equipment, working individually and with others, in one or more environments, in and around school or parks, woodlands, and the sea-shore.

OAA as a Programme of Study within the PE curriculum may, for many schools and teachers, be the least familiar activity area, even a new experience and teachers will need additional help and support through good, detailed curriculum documentation and staff development support, both informal and formal. The inclusion of OAA in the NC requirements indicates the value placed on providing pupils with experiences beyond the gym' or hall but outside of the classroom in challenging situations. Balazick (1995) believes:

> ❢ . . . *such activities will call on the individual to overcome physical and emotional difficulties, work with and trust others, and develop a respect for the natural world.* (p. 4)

OAA is no longer a requirement at Key Stage 1, but this should not deter you from promoting the activities as they will fulfil some of the general requirements for PE, as well as elements of the Programme of Study for Key Stage 1 Geography. Teachers working with Key Stage 2 pupils and in middle schools will have to deliver OAA — it is a statutory requirement.

This Programme of Study is not simply about 'doing' outdoor pursuits, it is a vital aspect of outdoor education in general, which The National Association for Outdoor Education (1970) defines as a means of approaching education objectives through guided, direct experience in the environment, using its resources as learning materials. Through such activities children learn to overcome physical and psychological challenges: for many this involves 'risk', which in turn implies 'danger', and many teachers will need reassurance that it is 'acceptable risk' and learn to manage such risk in order to create a safe learning environment (see Chapter 6 for further discussion in this area). It is worth noting once again that your programme for OAA should be written so that it can be delivered by non-specialist teachers without recourse to extensive and expensive INSET to satisfy LEA and DfEE and Health and Safety Codes of Practice.

While many outdoor and adventurous activities can be undertaken as part of the normal school timetable (for example, during a 45 minute lesson), others can be planned with a more flexible approach to timetabling.

The Suffolk County Council Guidelines (1992) offer suggestions particularly relevant to organising Key Stage 2 activities.

Offsite Visits — a whole or half day off-site visit provides opportunity for pupils to undertake, for example, an orienteering activity in a local park or woodland, or a water-sports session at a local water-sports centre. A full-day journey, involving pupils in both the planning and follow-up, is strongly recommended in Years 5 or 6.

An Activity Day — devote one day, or half day, to a carousel of activities on the school site for all pupils from one or more year groups. A number of staff can be involved, with ancillary help recruited for the day. Because they will be utilised several times by different groups, there is a more worthwhile return on the effort involved in setting up each of the activities. Schools might wish to consider this as an effective way of offering some of the outdoor challenge activities which might be difficult to include within the confines of the normal timetable.

A Topic Approach — Schools that use a topic approach to the delivery of part of the curriculum at Key Stage 2 may find scope to include aspects of OAA within topic headings. A topic on 'water' could obviously include some water-based outdoor activities, while camping and bivouacking might relate to a topic on homes and homelessness. One Suffolk school has successfully integrated a variety of adventurous activities into a Year 6 study of their local area.

A Pupil-directed Programme in Orienteering — . . . in orienteering, a programme of activities on the school site could be devised, relying on permanently marked control sites and prepared worksheets, through which pupils could progress at their own pace.

An Overnight Camp — An overnight camp or bivouac on the school field or local site is strongly recommended as an activity for pupils towards the end of Key Stage 2. . . . Staff ratios can be enhanced by splitting the year group and repeating the event on different evenings, and by involving parents. Although these extended activities do rely on the goodwill of teachers.

A Residential Course — . . . much of the Programme of Study at Key Stage 2 can be delivered through a single residential experience, although it would be sad to see this as a replacement for a progressive programme of activity throughout the Key Stage. It does offer opportunities to undertake more challenging activities in a more interesting environment, as the culmination of an ongoing programme of study.

(amended from *Suffolk County Council Guidelines*, 1992, pp. 24–5)

Swimming

Perhaps of all the activities, swimming for me is the most important. Having confidence and competence in and around water can help to save not only your own life but that of others. Inability to swim can limit, even exclude, children's involvement in other water-based activities — wind-surfing, canoeing, sailing, surfing, etc., often popular holiday pursuits.

The swimming Programme of Study focuses on the principles of water safety and survival, developing pupils' confidence in the water, how to rest, float, and support oneself in the water, effective and efficient swimming strokes on the front and back, and to be able to swim, unaided, competently and safely, for at least 25 metres.

Some general principles to establish in PE

Physical education and sport: What is the relationship between physical education and sport in your school curriculum?

The relationship between PE and sport has long been the subject of debate. To many people the terms are synonymous, but others see the two as quite distinct areas. To me, physical education and sport are not the same, yet they can work closely together in partnership.

Sport is about the physical, it covers a wide range of activities, and is usually associated with *competitive* games. The professional nature of sport is very visible and receives a high profile in the media, thus providing many children and adults with role models. Participation in sport is voluntary and is governed by the Sports Council, National Governing Bodies and the Central Council for Physical Recreation. It has its own coaching structure and network.

Physical education is also about the physical and covers the six prescribed activities previously discussed. It is an integral part of the total education process, and the emphasis is on *learning* and a process whereby children develop skills, knowledge and understanding, through competitive and cooperative experiences. It is not high profile and is often seen as a marginal subject in the school curriculum. It is compulsory, however, and is part of the statutory school curriculum. It is influenced by the British Association of Advisers and Lecturers in PE and the Physical Education Association UK.

Recent moves towards school and community links, see page 93, have accepted the differences and yet promoted recognition of the similarities between PE and sport (DES, 1989; DES, 1991): much has been done to promote integration (Murdoch, 1990) and 'partnerships'.

Competition versus cooperation: What is the place of competition in your school physical education curriculum?

The 1980s witnessed some controversial debates about the nature of *competition* in PE. Some schools of thought questioned its value and claimed that it promoted an elitist ideology. In those schools who adopted a 'win at all costs' attitude and preserved PE for the development of school teams, competition may well have been detrimental to children's welfare. Publicity to such a view generated a shift towards the opposite end of the continuum, focusing on *cooperation*. Such a reaction led to a dramatic decline of competition in school PE. However, competition per se is not unhealthy. Competition should be seen as an *integral* part of many activities, as it is in real life. Pupils of all abilities should experience a balanced programme where they experience and learn to manage competitive situations.

Cross-curricular work

Physical education should form an integral part of cross-curricular planning as it has much potential for establishing *genuine* links with other subjects. We need to not only look at the contribution PE can make to learning about other subjects but what other subjects can contribute to learning about PE. Aspects of PE can virtually link with every subject in the curriculum — particularly through topic work.

How can you manage cross-curricular work?

As cross-curricular matters are a whole school issue, establishing links will involve you consulting and working with other coordinators. The aim must be to design a coherent curriculum that offers children a rich variety of experiences that contribute to their overall development.

Make sure that the cross-curricular links are explicit and reasonably strong, so that both children and teachers must appreciate them — tenuous links will just fade and become non-existent.

Strong cross-curricular themes include:

Family/Home	Toys/Toy Shop	Clothes	Water	Time
Ourselves	Colours	Food	Seasons	Energy
Shape and Size	Seasons	Festivals	Weather	Machines
Olympics	The Farm	Space	Fireworks	The Romans

There are many opportunities in PE to establish cross-curricular links with other subjects:

- **Health Education and Science** — an emphasis on promoting healthy lifestyles offers opportunities to develop children's understanding about the benefits and effects of exercise on how the body works (science). Children can also learn about the effects of a lack of exercise, poor hygiene, poor diet.
- **Personal Social Education** — pupils can develop skills like self-discipline, the ability to work alone and with others in cooperative and competitive situations, and an understanding of fair play. Knowledge can be applied in practical situations.

Suggestion

Carry out a PE curriculum audit. What is currently taught? Are pupils receiving the National Curriculum entitlement? How well does your school programme meet the requirements? Are you meeting the requirements? If not, why not? What needs to be changed? How can you set about changing it?

What documentation is available? What happens in practice? Does the rhetoric match reality? How do you deal with progression and continuity between units of work and different year groups? Are activities taught in a progressive way? Is there consistency across the school or is there unnecessary repetition?

- **Safety** — learning how to handle equipment, follow rules, importance of warm-up and responding to instructions.
- **Athletics** — opportunities to measure, record and compare performance (mathematics).
- **Outdoor and adventurous activities** — pupils can develop environmental awareness (geography).
- **Dance** — making use of ideas and imagination to communicate feelings, moods and a message (English).
- **IT** — handling information related to measurement of personal and team performance, timing and the use of different software to help analyse results.

Physical education also offers numerous opportunities to reinforce:

Communication skills — different forms of expression, describing and analysing their own and others' performance; to use movement as a stimulus for creative work in language. Language codes and symbols used in different activities, the use of words.

Numeracy — teaching numbers many schools already use measuring distances, keeping personal records and analysing differences, progress, comparisons.

Observation skills — evaluating performance.

Expressive skills — dance is often taught alongside music and drama. Pupils may experience rhythm through movements; dance may provide a stimulus for composing; music may provide a stimulus for the creation and performance of a dance. Interpretation of Art work, paintings and sculptures as a stimulus.

Progression and continuity in PE

One of the main aims of the National Curriculum was to provide the basis for a common curriculum for all pupils. It was designed to highlight and promote continuity in the curriculum and in pupils' progress by establishing:

- common entitlement (in terms of subject studies) from Key Stage 1 to Key Stage 4;
- a clear definition of the content;
- common standards and assessment related to End of Key Stage Descriptors;

■ common vocabulary to facilitate planning for continuity in curricular provision and for describing pupils' progress from ages 5–16.

The End of Key Stage Descriptors define progression by identifying expectations, but the difficulty for teachers is the absence of any detailed guidance in the form of levels and associated statements of achievement. This places the responsibility for planning progression in the hands of the school, the PE coordinators and individual teachers. In some areas, groups of coordinators and teachers have got together to design and share schemes of work. This need for continuity, progression and sequencing of learning applies not only to lessons and units of work, between classes, year groups and Key Stages within schools, but also between schools and teachers nationally. It will promote consistency. But continuity and progression are not new concerns, in 1931 the Hadow Report recognised:

> ❛ . . . that the process of education from five to the end of the secondary stage, should be envisaged as a coherent whole. That there should be no sharp edges between infant, junior and post primary stages, and that transition from one stage to the succeeding stage should be as smooth and as gradual as possible. (DES, 1931, p. x)

Physical Education has responded to the various moves for coherence, continuity and progression by establishing a solid base of guidance material focusing on schemes of work and exemplars of good practice. However, the impact on widespread continuity and progression has been limited. In 1991, the HMI inspection review, *The Teaching and Learning of Physical Education*, reported that one of the factors contributing to the underachievement of pupils in the subject was a lack of progression in the work throughout the school. This section will firstly look at progression and continuity in relation to your school curriculum and then look at the issues related to transfer between primary and secondary schools. The first stage is to clarify what is already going on in your school.

From my discussions with colleagues it is apparent that continuity and progression are often seen as synonymous

Suggestion

What is progression and what is continuity? Spend a few minutes thinking about what you see as the key issues to do with progression and how your school curriculum and practice endeavours to promote it. Thinking about specific examples should help focus your thinking about what is already going on. Having done this you now need to think about other colleagues. How familiar are they with progression and continuity? How wide spread is your practice?

terms and frequently used interchangeably. This is not suprising since to achieve continuity one would expect to achieve progression and vice versa. However, there is a recognised difference. Continuity means a whole school approach, everyone speaking the same language and offering the same message. Keogh and Naylor (1993) suggest that while continuity is about communication between teachers, the emphasis in progression is more concerned with teacher–pupil interaction and what goes on in the classroom (p. 121). They also discuss 'matching' pupils' learning experiences, setting the right degree of challenge to deepen knowledge and lead to progression.

Other sources of reference provide us with similar interpretations. When reporting on the quality of education provided, OFSTED will look at the curriculum assessment provision and consider the question 'Is the curriculum planned effectively, providing continuity and progression of learning?' This will involve taking account not only of what is written down and what they see during the visit but what has gone on before and what will follow. It will involve looking at the quality of communication between teachers in terms of pupils' PE experiences. Evidence is needed on whether the PE curriculum builds systematically on previous experience and existing knowledge, understanding and skills.

> *Progression and continuity — this involves ensuring programmes of study, units of work and lesson plans link with each other and that tasks in individual lessons are logical, developmental and relate to each other. It involves pupils moving from dependence to independence, from the simple to more complex, looking at their own performance as well as that of others.* (...)

The Curriculum Council for Wales (1992) endorses such a view, as do BAALPE (1995) through its focus on safe practice:

> *... it is important that all pupils should follow the appropriate sequence of learning and its consolidation. Progression should take place when readiness on the part of the pupil is endorsed by the teacher as being safe and appropriate for that pupil.*
>
> (p. 36)

Furthermore BAALPE states:

 Continuity in learning is an important element in safe practice. Where pupils experience more than an intermittent break in their learning, teachers will need to give careful consideration to the reintroduction of those pupils to programmes of work which are implemented. In such circumstances, it may be necessary to revisit and to consolidate activities previously taken by the pupils before they progress further. Young people who move between schools and join classes as new pupils need special consideration in this regard. (p. 36)

To promote continuity and progression, therefore, it is important that your PE curriculum is carefully thought out and sequentially planned. Cohen (1987) and Siedentop (1991) discuss the importance of 'instructional alignment' in teaching and learning, that is, the need for teachers to 'match' intended outcomes, instructional processes and instructional assessment. This simply means you need to plan in such a way that the tasks you set your pupils match your original goals or objectives, and that the assessment of pupils' learning matches the objectives set and the instruction provided. Siedentop (1991) refers to this as procedural task analysis. He recommends that after establishing unit objectives, planning of the unit is developed by '. . . working backwards from the final performance description to where the unit begins' (p. 289). This is something that you, as PE coordinator, will have to manage. Further guidance on planning in this way is presented in Part 3. The same principles apply to the teaching of specific aspects and individual elements of learning, thus breaking down a particular skill or unit of performance into a series of events (for example, the progressions related to learning how to throw and catch and to take weight on hands as in a handstand).

Progression in games

Chedzoy (1996) dicusses the important principles about progression when teaching games. She uses the work of Thorpe (1990) to illustrate the need to plan, from the learning of simple net games to more complex invasion games.

Williamson (1993) similarly outlines a series of progressive stages to the development of games.

Stage 1 Identify the main principles of play of the three groups of games, allowing for differences between individual games within the group (netball and rugby are both invasion games using space but in different ways).

Stage 2 As far as possible place each principle in order of priority for teaching purposes (e.g. the simple exploitation of space on a tennis or badminton court is likely to be taught before the idea of short/long placement or use of angles).

Stage 3 Place this order of teaching in a 'timeline' (e.g. the principles to be covered in Year 2 will be less sophisticated than those in Year 5).

Stage 4 Identify appropriate games and practices which will help children to learn the principle of play (e.g. 4 versus 3 games to encourage the use of the 'extra' player, or changing the size of the target to encourage pupils to make decisions about appropriate attacking and defensive tactics).

Stage 5 Identify the specific skill/techniques they will need to learn in order to take part in the games/practices at an appropriate level (e.g. less able pupils learning about 'hitting to spaces', in fielding/striking games they may need to use longer bats and throw and hit a ball themselves, or even stimulate the hitting by an underarm roll or throw; more able pupils may be able to cope with a bowler or pitcher with regulation equipment. For these pupils the skills required are more extensive and sophisticated).

Stage 6 The written scheme of work should indicate that the main purpose of teaching is to help pupils understand principles of play and tactics. Techniques and skills are used as a means to achieve this end in the context of the game. They still have to be taught but when the need arises, e.g. when a pupil or teacher recognises the need to learn or teach a particular skill in order for the player to take part in the framework effectively.

Why are progression and continuity important?

It would be easy to say because it is good practice, but what are some of the specific reasons for you and your colleagues? When addressing this issue it would be worth spending a few minutes brainstorming responses. Some responses might include: duplication, developmental learning, pupils' motivation, coverage of the National Curriculum, establishing a whole school approach and a sense of shared purpose, reinforcing previous learning.

Duplication

A progressive curriculum will avoid pupils revisiting the same material. I was recently in a school where teachers from both the primary sector and the secondary sector met for the first time. It was interesting to note that they had no idea of what each other were doing and an examination of the curriculum documentation clearly indicated duplication was taking place.

Developmental learning

If learning is both to build on previous experiences and make the most of pupils' potential then material has to carefully structured, rather like a series of related building blocks. Many individual skills also have clearly laid out progressive steps to learning.

Pupils' motivation

Pupils need to be challenged and extended. Providing pupils with progressive materials will help to keep them involved and switched on. Differentiated learning opportunities will also help motivate pupils of different abilities to achieve and keep involved.

National Curriculum Coverage

Provision must be balanced and promote a common understanding regarding learning.

Whole school approach

This helps provide a sense of shared purpose and goals.

So, why hasn't it happened already?

Ensuring progression and continuity seems sensible and necessary if pupils' learning experiences are to be of value. However inspection evidence suggests that the impact of recent thinking and actions has been limited. There are many reasons for this and these are not dissimilar to those discussed by Keogh and Naylor (1993) when looking at developments in science.

Different priorities

Primary schools have faced dramatic change in recent years, this coupled with implementing National Curriculum PE has sidelined real developments in this area. It is also just another thing to do!

Difficulties associated with developing a shared view

This was reflected by HMI who reported: 'A major hindrance to progression and continuity was a failure to share professional ideas regularly. Where approaches had been agreed by teachers, there was often better progression in the work between age groups, and the potential of each child was more effectively developed' (HMI, 1991, p. 12).

Within schools there is a limited amount of time for formal and informal contact to discuss and share ideas on curriculum planning and delivery. There is even less time for teachers to observe each others' good practice. Effective time management has to be a central issue in making continuity and progression an integral part of whole school curriculum development.

Autonomy

Professional autonomy is highly valued and moving towards continuity between teachers can seem a threat to teachers' autonomy. However, the pupils' learning experiences must surely be given some priority whilst endeavouring to preserve a teacher's natural flair and personal approach.

Idealism

Progression and continuity can easily appear 'idealistic' and appear to demand extensive and detailed planning. An important strategy is to secure short manageable targets which will help teachers to work towards the 'ideals'.

When looking at progression on a daily or annual basis it is important that written schemes and learning materials are flexible enough to cater for children at different stages of physical, cognitive, social and emotional development. Cooper (1995) encourages us to refer to the progression principles of difficulty, variety and quality, focusing on small incremental progressions, providing practice and repetition as a means to progressive learning in all our lessons.

Progression — different levels

Planning for progression and continuity requires a vision of where you want PE to go in your school. Your scheme of work will represent your attempt to put this vision into action. The example scheme and units in Part Three (p. 152) illustrate such vision currently being recommended and implemented in different authorities.

Continuity between primary and secondary schools

As coordinator you must be concerned with progression not only in your own school curriculum, but also between upper junior pupils and their secondary school. This will inevitably involve collaboration between primary and secondary colleagues and the setting up of partnerships to ensure a smooth and relatively straightforward transfer (see pp. 93–4), and will enable you to:

■ take stock of existing arrangements which have evolved over the years;
■ evaluate the effectiveness of the curriculum arrangements to support continuity;
■ develop professional links between the schools.

In areas where primary schools transfer the majority of their pupils to a single secondary school, and where secondary schools receive pupils from a few primary schools, the practicalities of transfer procedures and the development of professional links can be pretty straightforwad. However, for many areas, the transfer between the Key Stages is more complex and requires close liaison. Evidence from OFSTED continues to show that continuity between primary and secondary is inappropriate, so much so that SCAA have produced guidance to help schools audit existing arrangements, develop effective and manageable procedures to support pupils' transfer and improve the professional links between associated schools (1996b). This is very useful for the development of a school policy which in turn should influence your school's practice in PE.

Extra-curricular provision (ECP)

It is recognised and expected practice that all schools should provide a programme of extra-curricular activities which complement the formal curriculum. But why? Physical education has always held education for leisure (pre-1980s) as one of its objectives; more recently this has become known as preparation for lifelong participation. Sport also contributes to the general ethos of the school, and well-planned programmes can make a significant contribution to the social and moral education of young people through valuable recreational and competitive activities.

Extra-curricular provision received particular emphasis in the government policy *Sport Raising the Game 1995* which promoted the phrase 'putting sport at the heart of school life' (p. 2). Not only did this endorse the idea of offering children opportunities to continue with sport outside formal lessons, but also of rewarding teachers who make such additional commitment with additional salary points, at the discretion of the governing body. This was a much needed move, but it increased the demands on primary school colleagues whose existing heavy workload leaves very little time for yet more work in what may be perceived as a less important area of the curriculum. You will need to give serious consideration to using parents, outside agencies and clubs to maximise opportunities.

It is worth noting that the good practice noted by OFSTED (1995) was characterised by the time devoted by staff; good range and quality of provision; equality of opportunity; high participation rates; and liaison with schools and other agencies. More importantly the most significant influence on the volume, range and quality of the programmes offered in primary schools was you, the subject coordinator.

This document highlighted the role of OFSTED in monitoring the range and quality of both formal and extra-curricular provision. In particular they will

(a) inspect and report on the range, time spent and quality of games, including competitive team games, offered as part of the formal curriculum;

(b) report on sporting provision that schools offer to pupils outside formal lessons, during lunchtimes, in the evenings and at weekends, paying particular attention to traditional team games;

(c) report on pupil participation rates in sporting provision outside formal lesson time and the number of teachers who supervise that provision;

(d) report on the school's sports competition programme, both within the school and against other schools; and

(e) report on the progress made by the school in improving provision in both curricular and extra-curricular competitive games as part of this sporting initiative.

This monitoring complements the existing OFSTED framework for the inspection of primary schools, and could lead to a school being granted Sportsmark Award. This scheme rewards schools who offer at least four hours per week of structured sport outside the formal curriculum. The scheme's emphasis on games, and competitive games, is rather irritating but nevertheless the much needed recognition of this element of PE is to be welcomed.

In some schools, lunchtime ECP serves as a management strategy to keep children's behaviour under control. Indeed, OFSTED (1995) reported that one of the most important features of extra-curricular physical activity was through 'lunchtime organiser' arrangements. This involved every class having a lunchtime organiser whose duty it is to ensure that games are available in a systematic and orderly way for pupils of all ages. Whilst this provision is to be commended it did cost £23,000 per year, well beyond the means of many schools. However, according to the school observed it was a worthy investment in terms of organised learning and well-managed behaviour at lunchtime.

In the past, extra-curricular provision has usually focused on the running of school teams for inter- and intra-school competitions. Recent initiatives have encouraged schools to offer more recreational activities, thus promoting lifelong participation and PE as a leisure activity (OFSTED, 1996). This raises two questions: What strategies can your school adopt to increase the participation rate of pupils in extra-curricular physical activity? Since the provision for extra-curricular sporting activity for boys is significantly better than for girls, how can the gender imbalance of opportunity be addressed?

You need to consider these issues during your own review of provision. For ease I have organised the review into three tasks which relate to assessing and improving the quality of your provision. They involve looking at what is on offer, increasing your awareness of the expectations of recognised good practice, and identifying things to do to for improvement!

What extra-curricular programme is currently available in your school?

As coordinator you should be actively involved in the design and delivery of the school's extra-curricular programme. The size of your school and available resources will shape the type of programme you are able to offer and it is important that the programme you offer is within your resources and meets the needs of your pupils. In some cases it may be necessary to try and establish links with other schools to extend the range and availability of resources.

The first stage is to look at your policy for ECP. What does it say? Does it reflect commitment to a broad and balanced programme for all pupils? Does the statement reflect your identified 'aims' for PE? Is the statement related to actual practice? Figure 4.1 outlines the policy statement for Avondale Middle School. How does this compare to your own school's policy? What do you think the statement tells you about the school's approach to extra-curricular provision? Compare the content with the OFSTED criteria for good practice on page 119. If you do not have an explicit statement, you could use Figure 4.1 as a model.

During my interviews with PE coordinators they generally indicated limited staff support for offering ECP. Laura outlined how at her school ECP revolves around rugby and netball and that when talking about involving other members of staff, 'some would help . . . well, they would do a favour for me really, no one volunteers'. It is a similar case for Jane who recognised that few teachers had any real interest to stay behind after school, 'There is so much to do with your class that extra PE is the last thing on peoples' minds. Sorting out what to do for PE and game is difficult enough without extra!'

Suggestion

Complete a timetable outlining what activities children do during the lunchtime and after school? Are these activities for all children? How many members of staff are involved? How many children are regularly involved?

91

FIG 4.1

Avondale middle school physical education policy for extra-curricular provision

Our ethos on extra-curricular provision at Avondale is quite simple — we try to provide as many opportunities for as many of our pupils to take part in sports activities outside of school hours. We aim to balance this between competitive fixtures for teams, and recreational opportunities. All our provision depends on willing helpers in terms of staff, parents and former pupils.

Guidance for staff

It is policy that at no time should anyone other than a teacher have sole responsibility for an extra-curricular activity. This means that if a parent has volunteered to run a club then the teacher in charge must be present on site — preferably on the field or at least in the school building. The role of the non-qualified person should be ideally as an assistant to the teacher in charge, although we are fortunate here to have some very experienced parent coaches who are more than competent to organise children effectively. As a general rule the afore mentioned should stand. Where possible we try to avoid cancelling a club for a fixture, but since our staffing is small there will be occasions where the main teacher will be called away to attend a match, and may have no alternative but to cancel the club. We regret this situation but hope that in the fullness of time a solution may be found.

On the issue of cancelled clubs, we aim to always inform the children a day in advance by way of a note in registers. Should the club be cancelled on the day — for an urgent reason or severe weather — then we endeavour to inform the children personally as early on in the day as possible. All staff involved are encouraged to ask another member of staff to cover a club before cancelling. Registers should be kept of the numbers and names that attend the clubs so that we may monitor our effectiveness. The person responsible for the club should take charge for ensuring that all equipment is returned in good order, and that there are no children left alone after the club has finished.

Guidance for children

We ask children to make firm arrangements for travelling home from our charge. Should they be intending to walk home, then we insist that they are appropriately 'covered up'. Their parents are expected to pick them up at the time the club or fixture is due to finish. If they are involved in a fixture, then a permission slip will be issued to the child, days in advance for the parents to sign. The teacher in charge is responsible for collecting the signed slips.

We ask our children to make a regular commitment to our clubs, especially if they are interested in representing the school in a team. We reserve the right to exclude a child from a team, however talented, if they have made no effort to commit to a club.

We do not insist on PE kit in club situations, just that the children are appropriately dressed for the activity. However, for school representation they are required to wear school kit.

Every term we aim to provide inter-form competitions in major sports for all year groups.

These involve all classes fielding teams to compete against each other in their own year group.

This allows the keen children who may not be able to gain a place in the school team to compete for a trophy.

For more details of team selection etc. please refer to the main policy document.

It may be possible to recruit a few colleagues to get involved, firstly during the lunchtime and occasionally after school, but there is no need to solely rely on colleagues. The move towards partnership in provision encourages us to look towards involving parents and others working in sport in the local community. It might even be possible to set-up a joint initiative with other local primary schools or even with your link secondary school. (Be aware of the 'duty of care' which extends to all ECP and the red tape that surrounds transport, insurance, first aid, you need to be well covered for all eventualities.) This all takes planning time, so take care not to set yourself too many targets. Identify ECP as one element of your subject development plan and each year take another step forward.

Partnership with parents and the community

Since the mid-1980s there has been a great shift towards schools working more closely with their local community. This was particularly prominent in PE following the *School Sport Forum: Partnership in Action* (1988) initiative which stated:

 schools cannot be expected to take entire responsibility for the provision of sporting opportunities for young people; other agencies must be involved. (p. 7)

Suddenly there was recognition that parents and other people involved in sport could and should work together with schools in order to not only maximise opportunities for young people, but also maximise the use of existing facilities. After all, why should school facilities lay idle throughout the weekend, during holiday times and after 5 o'clock. Furthermore why shouldn't pupils have the opportunity to visit local facilities and make use of them for curriculum and extra-curricular activities.

This movement towards partnership has continued to develop and gain momentum and it now appears as part of the common requirements of the statutory curriculum for pupils at Key Stage 3:

Suggestion

Think of the local community within a 10, 15 and 20 kilometre radius. Who could be possible partners?
Parents: are any experienced sports people and/or qualified coaches? Every school is likely to have some parents with particular skills or interests that could be employed or deployed.
Local schools: what expertise could be shared with other primary and/or secondary schools? What are other schools doing, how can you share ideas and create a supportive network?
Local sports organisations will be able to provide a valuable source of information, ideas resources, expertise and possibly have under-used facilities which may be made available.

> *Throughout the key stage, pupils should be given opportunities to engage in health-promoting physical activity, where possible within the local community.* (DFE, 1995, p. 6)

Whilst this does not specifically refer to Key Stages 1 and 2, I believe many youngsters can join different activity clubs during their primary years — gymnastics, swimming, dance, tennis and football to name just a few — and there is no reason why we shouldn't promote this practice as early as possible. Furthermore, OFSTED have looked at how, through PE, the school can encourage and work with parents to support children's learning; actively promote partnership between the school and home; establish clear lines of communication; and develop a variety of approaches to relations with parents (OFSTED, 1995, p. 97).

There are a number of different types and levels of schemes, so deciding what is best for your school is important. Whatever scheme is implemented it is important that the school and their governing bodies have a key role in the planning process (NCC, 1991; SSF, 1988) and that any partnership schemes are coordinated and systematically developed.

Managing partnership schemes — what and how?

Partnership schemes have taken all sorts of forms and levels. Three broad levels were offered in the National Curriculum proposals for PE:

> *as providers of information: the school simply passes on information about opportunities for activities, leaving the children to make the decisions about whether to participate;*
>
> *as providers of complementary provision: the school provides access to other opportunities, e.g. taster sessions, thus offering direct contact and advise;*
>
> *working together with outside agencies: involves the schools and agencies working cooperatively to plan and deliver opportunities. Joint initiatives are a key feature.* (DES, 1991, p. 67)

One fundamental principle when designing partnerships is that, in the school context, teachers should take the lead and

Think about

What types of partnership you are already offering. How well are these are working? How can you extend what is currently going on to increase future opportunities?

remember that whenever others are involved the school teacher stills holds responsibility in *loco parentis*.

If you haven't really focused on this area before you may be surprised about how much you are probably already doing as a matter of good practice. The following are examples of the different levels of partnership, which you may find useful.

- Noticeboards can be used to display details of local and regional activities with contact addresses, additional information, etc. Encourage children to take notice of particular events, especially those available after school, at weekends and during the holidays.
- Sports directories can be made available to pupils giving general information about sports outside of school (these could be drawn up by a group of schools within the same locality).
- Special afternoon or day when parents, coaches and representatives from local clubs come into school and promote their activities. This may involve some creative timetabling or be part of a theme for the week.
- Visits by pupils to local clubs as part of the curriculum or out-of-school hours, for information, coaching and playing.
- Pupils can be given opportunities to do National Governing Body (NGB) awards.

Use of outside facilities

Many schools already make good use of local sporting facilities, particularly the local swimming pool. This serves as a good introduction to these facilities and can help to break down any barriers that they may have about who can use them, how to use them, procedures involved, etc. When working in such places teachers may involve outside staff and this can be a good way of offering children specialist tuition. Staff may also share ideas, perhaps learn some new ideas.

Dual use is a more detailed partnership scheme which can involve various approaches. For example joint provision, shared use or community schools.

When facilities are located in a school, and designed and funded by the school and a non-education source it is known as joint provision. Both funding partners are involved from the outset and participate in the management arrangements.

Schools identified as 'community schools' are defined in the Education Reform Act 1988 as schools where non-school activities take place on the premises, under the management or control of the governing body. Initiatives could include community organisations, adult evening classes or Youth groups. This type of scheme is very similar to 'shared use' where facilities originally designed and provided for school use have subsequently been made available for community use.

In 1991 The Sports Council provided a very useful guide *A Sporting Double: School and Community*, to help governors and teachers introduce and extend dual use schemes in their schools. If you consider there to be potential in moving in this direction it would offer some good guidance. It includes a video which could be used to involve all staff.

All of the above initiatives not only help to generate enthusiasm and reinforce sport in schools but may also help lead pupils to continue taking part in sport outside school hours.

Recommendations for setting up partnerships

All schools will need to decide what is the most appropriate partnership scheme for their community. In PE this will involve analysing what you need, what is available and the approach most suitable for your particular circumstances. Before you start, decide which type of partnership is most appropriate for the needs of your school. You will need to define:
- what are the needs and priorities of the teachers and children in the school?
- how may developing partnerships benefit the children and the staff, individually and collectively?
- what are the gaps in the provision (facilities/teaching/training) within the school?

■ what are the possibilities or opportunities for external partnerships and community provision? which one may best fit your needs?

Look at your strengths and how they can be shared as well as identify areas where you offer only limited opportunities. Then find out what partnership opportunities are available locally, regionally and nationally.

Chapter 5   Effective teaching and learning in PE

Effective teaching of PE is no different to any other subject. It is the content and the environment that makes PE different. But effective learning requires good teaching regardless of the subject. This involves teachers using a variety of methods and styles and knowing how and when to use them. In the past PE has often been criticised for being too games orientated, elitist, with an overemphasis on didactic teaching all of which often alienated many children. Consequently during the mid-1980s the debate on good practice in PE focused on the *process* of learning, with an emphasis on how children were engaged in lessons. This took some of the emphasis away from the content, product, and the discussion became 'process versus product'. However, the two issues are not in fact separable from each other and the National Curriculum recognised the importance of both.

Process revolves around making 'experiences' an important part of learning, relevant and enjoyable. Mawer (1990), when discussing Teaching Skills in Physical Education, suggested 'It's not what you do — it's the way that you do it' (p. 307), and this recognises that good practice has more to do with style than with content. Like many others, I believe good style elevates teaching above the level of drill and rote. It captures the fleeting regard of students, holds their attention, grabs their interest, entertains them, and wins their enduring confidence (Stephens and Crawley, 1994). But PE is also different in that it takes place in large spaces, often open, visible and subject to changes in the weather. Teachers will need confidence to use their existing teaching skills in these different, often more demanding, environments.

The ideas and discussion presented in this chapter are derived from practising teachers and working with coordinators and consultants who promote the development of knowledge about effective teaching and learning in PE. Several tasks are suggested to help you as the coordinator develop your own thinking, bring you up-to-date with national guidance and how you can share this with your colleagues.

What is effective teaching?

Over recent years there has been considerable interest in the need to define 'good teaching', 'effective teaching', 'teaching competence'. Despite this interest there is no definitive checklist and the language used to define effective teaching will largely depend on the writers and their purpose. For example, Wragg (1984) recognised the difficulty in trying to define 'teaching skill' and described it as problematic due to the varied nature of the job:

> Pressing the right button on a tape recorder, or writing legibly on the blackboard require but modest competence, and are things most people could learn with only a little practice. Responding to a disruptive adolescent, or knowing how to explain a difficult concept to children of different ages and abilities by choosing the right language, appropriate examples and analogies, and reading the many cues which signal under-standing or bewilderment, requires years of practice as well as considerable intelligence and insight.
> (p. 7)

In this sense teaching is not just about being able to respond to pupils, but knowing the right response according to the pupils' needs: it requires a teacher's experience and personal qualities to interact with pupils' differing personal situations. This contrasts with DfE requirements that all newly qualified primary teachers are expected to have by the end of Initial Teacher Training: Circular 14/93 declares a portfolio of professional competencies related to: *Curriculum Content, Planning and Assessment* (whole curriculum; subject knowledge and application; assessment and recording of pupils' progress); *Teaching Strategies* (pupils' learning; teaching strategies and techniques); and *Further Professional Development*. These are to be superseded by the Standards for the Award of Qualified Teacher Status (1997) which identifies the following key competencies: subject knowledge and understanding; planning, teaching and class management; monitoring, assessment, recording, reporting and accountability; other professional requirements. These designated competencies form the main criteria against which teaching skills will be assessed, but they tell us little about the personal qualities a teacher brings to the classroom. Furthermore, the demands on Initial Teacher Education are such that many student-teachers experience courses in PE of anything ranging from 20 hours to 120 hours; with a National Curriculum offering six areas of experience this provision can surely only scratch the surface of developing competence to deliver PE. A Newly Qualified Teacher's Profile is also designed to add to this list of expected areas of competence and this, coupled with the OFSTED guidance to inspectors for assessing the quality of teaching (1995), outlined on page 119, provides schools with useful criteria as a guide for evaluating lessons and planning staff development.

But are all subjects the same? Do some subjects require specific teaching skills and competencies for effective teaching? Much of the research in PE has focused on teaching secondary PE, but primary teachers can draw and learn from much of the evidence presented in national reports. The first report on PE, following the implementation of the National Curriculum, based its findings on inspection reports of 105 primary schools and concluded the most successful teaching was characterised by

> ❟ *. . . well-planned lessons with clear learning objectives. The teachers used constructive comment well, and demonstrations were used effectively to improve the standard of the work. A good pace was set and time was used effectively. Good, safe practice was evident in the teachers' established routines.*

In 1995, OFSTED reported the following key features of high quality teaching and learning in secondary schools:

High quality teaching was always associated with high levels of pupil achievement. The best teaching . . . was seen in lessons that were well planned and had clear learning objectives, which were shared with the pupils. Good organisation, clear structure, high levels of activity, maintenance of good pace and well-judged use of a range of teaching styles made best use of the available teaching time. (p. 4)

The report acknowledged that most of these positive features were also evident in primary schools, however, they found that the quality was generally more variable since most classes were taught by non-specialists class teachers. This sort of information can always be printed out and put on the staff noticeboard, thus raising colleagues' awareness of recent information.

Mawer (1995) asked 23 heads of PE departments and advisers in local education authorities 'What do you consider to be the essential teaching skills of an effective teacher of physical education?' He calls this the professionals' view, summarised in Figure 5.1. My own interviews with primary teachers, coordinators and consultants indicate that

effective teaching is
- about KNOWING YOUR SUBJECT
- being ENTHUSIASTIC and passing this enthusiasm on to your pupils
- about PRESENTATION, making your subject exciting and relevant
- about KNOWING YOUR PUPILS and their world
- about DEVELOPING UNDERSTANDING, making complex issues easy.

Think about

What do you consider to be the essential characteristics of quality teaching and learning in Physical Education in your school? How well developed are these essential characteristics in all your teachers? You might like to conduct a staffing audit to identify known strengths, needs and concerns of you and your colleagues (a sample is outlined in Part One p. 50).

All of these 'teaching skills' are integral to your own role as a teacher, but a large part of your coordinator's work will involve you working with colleagues to develop their personal teaching skills thus preparing them to deliver effective, good quality PE.

Drawing on the various interpretations of teaching skills the remainder of this chapter examines some of the issues related to creating an effective learning environment.

FIG 5.1
Summary of Mawer's research findings into the essential skills of an effective PE teacher

Knowledge
    broad based knowledge of subject
    content knowledge
    of National Curriculum
    of school organisation
    of special events/Sports Day
Planning and Preparation
    in relation to National Curriculum programme of study
    safety issues
    differentiation of activities according to ability; equal opportunities
Organisation and Management
    safe use of equipment and resources
    class control and discipline
    time management
Teaching styles
    use of appropriate range of styles; pace and judgment
Communication skills
    clarity of expression
    effective use of voice
    ability to demonstrate
Observational skills
    able to analyse movement
    able to recognise skilful performance
    know what it is meant by quality in performance
    ability to assess pupils as a basis for progression
Miscellaneous skills mentioned
    adaptability
    interpersonal skills
    ability to self reflect
    cultural awareness

How can teachers create a positive learning atmosphere in PE?

How does the teacher set about creating an effective learning environment? What are the key issues? Will all teachers create the same environment? How do you prefer to teach PE? Do colleagues have preferences? Do you become excited or are you calm and quiet? Do you always use your whistle to get the children's attention or can you use your voice or give a hand signal? Teachers make decisions about what they are going to do and how they are going to organise themselves, the pupils, and the working environment. These decisions added together create the atmosphere for learning.

The teacher

The teacher must have good subject knowledge and an ability to interact and communicate with pupils and colleagues. Whilst excellent facilities, different teaching methods and potentially able children all contribute to high standards, the most single influencing factor is the teacher. Something I recall from my own teacher training is:

> *'The man is always more important than his method, his personality more important than his technique'*
>
> (Bilborough and Jones, 1973, p. 120)

The personal qualities of the teacher are clearly of primary importance. These relate to the example set by the teacher, through behaviour, appearance, effort, enthusiasm, integrity, approachability, sympathy — all are seen as desirable characteristics which reflect personality and charisma. In terms of the PE experience, however, it is also the teacher's philosophy, knowledge, understanding and teaching skills which directly influence the learning opportunities provided.

The teacher's subject knowledge has already been outlined as a significant factor in providing effective learning. Occasionally teachers may exclude certain activities from the PE programme because of lack of knowledge on the part of the teacher, this should not be acceptable practice. It can be avoided through monitoring and evaluation, the provision of INSET and staff development, and the sharing of ideas and experiences amongst staff (see Chapter 3 for further details).

There are various factors which will influence how teachers deliver their material:
- the learner (age/ability/gender/experience/preferred learning styles/);
- the learning objectives/outcomes;
- the lesson context (group size/teaching area/equipment);
- safety;
- teaching style.

Being aware and responding to these factors and how they shape the learning environment is a daily part of the teacher's role.

Teaching styles

Over the last decade the use of various teaching styles has gradually helped to change the process of PE — from pupils passively responding to teacher-led material to pupils actively being involved (Mosston, Ashworth, 1986, and Thorpe, 1990). This shift in the way material is delivered has had a dramatic effect on involving children not only in performance activities but also the planning and evaluation of work.

The development of the National Curriculum also encouraged more active pupil learning through an emphasis on performing, planning and evaluating. This undoubtedly influences the style of teaching to be employed which in turn will have an immediate effect on the organisation of the lesson. The broad spectrum of styles illustrated in Figure 5.2 shows the continuum of teacher activity from total control to that of facilitating children's independent working.

A rich mixture of teaching styles is needed to create an exciting and motivating learning environment. As objectives vary — for example, from developing individual motor skills to team work — so the effective teacher needs to be able to move easily from one style into another, adapting organisation and making use of a repertoire of teaching skills to create the right conditions for learning.

Command and practice styles of teaching are considered to be 'direct' teaching, where the teacher makes the decisions about the objectives, content, organisation and progressions. When using a command style of teaching the teacher is likely to focus on whole class teaching. This is particularly useful if
- there are any concerns about safety or discipline;
- an activity has to be taught to everyone or there is a need for uniformity;
- there is a shortage of time.

For teachers who are keen to monitor pupils' discipline and maintain close class control this is a very useful style. It is very formal and may be used when working towards certain objectives; for example, learning to take out equipment in an orderly manner, demonstrating, refining, assessing particular

Style	Essential characteristics	Likely objectives	Focus
A. Command	■ All decisions made by the teacher. ■ Learners do as they are told. ■ The class responds as a group.	■ Conformity to a single standard of performance. ■ Efficiency in the use of time to acquire skills. ■ Safety and discipline.	Motor development
B. Practice	■ Most decisions made by the teacher. ■ The learner makes some decisions at the impact stage. ■ A period of practice time on a task is set by the teacher, who can help individuals.	■ To improve skill. ■ To make learners aware of the relationship between commitment of time and quality of product or outcome. ■ To help learners to judge their level of performance.	Motor development
C. Reciprocal	■ Planned by teacher, executed by learners. ■ Learners work in pairs, one taking role of teacher and other of learner, roles are exchanged. ■ Clear criteria, generally on cards, are an integral part of this style. ■ The teacher gives responsibility for execution to pupils; works through pupil-teacher.	■ To engage pupils in social situations. ■ To develop communication skills. ■ To develop skills of observing, listening and analysing. ■ To heighten awareness of others, patience and tolerance. ■ To provide for maximum feedback from each performer.	Social (and motor) development
D. Self-check	■ Planned by teacher. Performance criteria essential. ■ Individuals check their own performance, i.e. make decisions at the impact stage. ■ Post-impact decisions made in relation to clearly stated criteria.	■ To help learners assess their own performance. ■ To help personal development in terms of honesty and the ability to be objective. ■ To help learners recognise their own limitations.	Personal (and motor) development
E. Inclusion	■ Planned by teacher. ■ Individuals check their own performance, starting at their own levels and progressing appropriately. ■ Tasks are set so that individual progress is highlighted.	■ To maximise involvement at appropriate levels of performance. ■ To accommodate individual differences. ■ To help learners rationalise their aspirations with reality. ■ To enable everyone to succeed.	Personal (and motor) development
All the above styles display teacher control at pre-impact stage			
F. Guided discovery	■ The teacher plans a target and systematically leads the learners to discover the target. ■ Questioning by the teacher is fundamental to this style. ■ The choice of the appropriate steps in the discovery process is critical to success. ■ Redirection of learners who go off at a tangent.	■ To engage learners in a convergent process of discovery. ■ To develop sequential discovery skills and consequences of action. ■ To develop patience while progressing through skilful matching of response to questions and stimuli.	Cognitive (and motor) development
G. Problem-solving (divergent)	■ The teacher presents questions or a problem situation, and pupils are invited to discover an alternative solution. ■ Frequently pupils are organised into groups to encourage shared thinking. ■ Pupils contribute to decisions at all stages since their response may determine the next move.	■ To develop the ability to work on problems and solve them. ■ To develop insights into the structure of an activity through the search for a solution. ■ To develop the ability to verify solutions. ■ To encourage independent thinking. ■ To promote learners' confidence in their own ideas and responses.	Cognitive and social (plus motor and personal) development
H. Individual programme	■ The learner plans and designs the programme. ■ The teacher proposes the subject matter and approves the programme.	■ To encourage independent planning and assessment under guidance. ■ To reveal the level of understanding through application. ■ To encourage persistence in completing a programme. ■ To promote self-confidence.	Cognitive and personal (plus motor) development
I. Learner initiatives	■ The learner selects the content, and plans and designs the programme with the approval of the teacher. ■ The learner executes the programme and submits an evaluation to the teacher.	■ To encourage and develop independence. ■ To display understanding through selection and application. ■ To encourage the acceptance of personal responsibility. ■ To develop self-confidence.	Cognitive and personal (plus motor) development
J. Self-teaching	The learner is both teacher and learner, working fully independently.		Cognitive, personal and motor development

(*Source*: BAALPE, 1989, pp. 12–13)

FIG 5.2
Styles of teaching

motor skills. Class organisation is usually regimented, in lines where everyone is looking at the teacher. But command-style teaching is not appropriate in all situations. If a lesson objective is to develop pupils' thinking skills or to provide pupils with opportunities for planning and evaluating their own and that of other work it would be very limited. It allows little opportunity for differentiation and treats everyone the same.

Teachers usually move from command into a practice style of teaching. They still maintain close control and make the decisions about lesson objectives, content organisation and progressions. The difference is that pupils will have some opportunity to work at their own pace, have more time to practise a task, to work at a more individual level and receive personal feedback. When moving into this style the teacher begins to accommodate pupil differences and encourage some element of pupil independence.

The practice style can lead to different forms of class organisation. Pupils can be organised to work in different groups on different tasks, make use of task sheets. It is particularly useful when equipment is limited. It also provides the teacher with time to interact with individuals, observe pupil progress and record their observations.

The spectrum of styles presented in Figure 5.2 illustrates the varying nature of the relationship between the teacher and the learner, particularly with an increasing emphasis on the learner becoming more responsible for, and involved in, the learning process. The BAALPE text *Teaching and Learning Strategies in Physical Education* (1989) offers a number of useful examples of how teachers tried and practised what they considered 'less familiar' even 'new' styles of teaching. The report strongly reflects the benefits of pupils' active involvement in the learning process.

 More children were actively involved, with greater participation.

The pupils were all totally involved in their lessons, and in my view their level of understanding games did improve.

Reciprocal teaching necessarily involved pupils in the cognitive skills of reading, interpreting, communicating, observing,

Suggestion

Look at your PE curriculum. What are the common teaching styles used? Take each Programme of Study and list the most common styles used in each area. Do some styles suit specific activities? Why? What factors do you feel affect the choice of teaching style? How can these factors be addressed?

Suggestion

Identify a lesson to be observed or make use of a video resource. Observe the lesson and identify how many teaching styles are used by the teacher. Discuss the findings and comment on the most common styles used. Did they provide the right opportunities for pupils to plan, perform and evaluate? Which styles were most effective? Why?

'To create a positive learning environment in PE takes time and, as in the classroom, good working routines need to be taught (they don't just happen).' (Rowe, 1996, p. 15)

analysing, evaluating and modifying the responses of their parents. (pp. 21, 15)

When using teaching styles where children assume more responsibility for their own learning, it is essential that they understand their role. Teachers will therefore need to initially explain to pupils why they are working in this particular way, and to link this with lesson objectives, so that they understand the process.

You will probably find that many teachers already use a range of teaching styles and strategies within their normal practice, but it is important that certain activities do not become linked to certain styles of teaching. Styles must be linked with performing, planning and evaluating in all activity areas. If you uncover a heavy reliance on selected teaching styles it may be appropriate to set up a workshop to specifically look at helping colleagues try out new ideas.

Organisation and management

Creating an effective learning environment requires good working routines and protocols. Teachers feel generally 'safe' in their own classrooms, but working with pupils in large PE spaces can be a challenge. The school should have an agreed policy which sets out agreed routines (management protocols) for all children, including:

- Moving from the classroom to the changing room.
- The routine when using the changing rooms.
- Housekeeping rules — non-participants, jewellery, accidents.
- Entering the work areas.
- Starting and stopping signals during a lesson.
- Using equipment — getting it out, using it and putting it away.
- Working in pairs, small groups or teams.
- Leaving the lesson.

All class teachers should receive a copy of this policy. They should be encouraged to spend time on establishing and reinforcing these routines so that they become part of normal practice and lead to the smooth running of PE lessons. We know that teachers like to be involved in school policy decisions so why not involve children in making the rules? Including children in discussions might help to create 'ownership' and help them understand the purpose of the rules. Children will need to be taught the routines, they will have to practise them and know that they will be expected to follow them during all PE lessons. In early PE lessons learning objectives may even include the learning of these routines rather than practical activities. Some rules could be posted on the classroom noticeboard or in the changing rooms as brief reminders for pupils and teachers.

HAVE FUN — BE SAFE! THINK ABOUT OTHERS THINK SAFE!

REMEMBER: YOU NEED YOUR PE KIT NO JEWELLERY UNSURE — ASK SOMEONE BE SAFE

As coordinator you should play a key role in designing, implementing and monitoring such protocols, which will help consistency and continuity as the children move up through the school.

The policy should also include guidance and strategies for teachers to use in the event of misbehaviour. Dealing with inappropriate behaviour is important and we should have short and long term strategies to cope with such events. Equally we should have some understanding about the different types and levels of misbehaviour; for example, it is rarely necessary to have total silence in a PE lesson, unless of course the task is to listen, either to the teacher or to another pupil.

Prolonged misbehaviour or more serious breach of protocol will require a whole school agreed policy on teacher action.

You may also wish to include schemes that encourage, acknowledge and reward 'good behaviour' in your policy. A successful school reward system will motivate children and promote mutual respect. It is important that 'on task' and 'good' behaviour is rewarded with appropriate praise: 'You've put a great deal of effort . . .', I was impressed by . . .', 'Well done . . .'. Assemblies, noticeboards, occasional treats (taking

Think about

What safety rules do you have?
How do you teach these rules to your classes?
What routines are in place?
How do pupils learn these routines?
Do the routines work?

'Don't let them wind you up. A smile and a beautiful remark to some little horror can completely disarm them for the whole lesson, they think you're wonderful even though you want to shout at them, and this could go well.'
(Mawer, 1995, p. 128)

the apparatus out/doing favourite activities), personal conversations all help to create a supportive working environment where children know that their efforts will be rewarded. Children also love to collect badges, stamps or any form of merit which makes them feel good. This is to be encouraged, providing any system is *linked with high expectations*.

Organising pupils for learning

Organising pupils into groups can be done in a variety of ways according to the activities taking place, the group size, the facilities and equipment available. Suggestions from the North Eastern Education and Library Board (NEELB) include:

> In a restricted area, half class working/half class observing.
> Individual work for ball familiarisation/specific dance step/specific gymnastic movement.
> In 2s for partner cooperation/competitive work, 'Follow the Leader', mirror work, etc.
> Trio work for e.g. unstructured group work.
> 4s for skill application, structured group work, small sided games etc.

From time to time classes will have to be arranged quickly into teams or groups of various numbers. According to the majority of teachers and colleagues interviewed, the most frequently used criteria for organising pupils into pairs or groups is 'friendship' through a common phrase 'find yourself a partner'. This method was considered to be the most effective because it is quick and because it is usually based on friendship it helps solve any social issues, but it can lead to arguments, popularity contests and disappointments. How effective is this for pupils' learning? Is it appropriate for pupils to work with their friends all of the time? What other ways could you and your colleagues organise pupils?

> A number of different strategies can be used to quickly organise pupils into working groups. These include:
> A class of 28 has to be grouped in 4s. Line children up and number them 1 to 7. All 'ones' form a group, 'twos', 'threes', etc.
> Alternatively number pupils 1, 2, 3 and 4 — these form a group.

Suggestion

Analyse the criteria used for pupil groupings. When organising a group what factors do you consider?
Spend about five minutes brainstorming.
Answers might include: ability, age, experience, gender, physique, race, resources, safety.
Which criteria dominate? Why?
Discuss why some strategies are never used — can/should they?

To get a balance of height, age or size the lines can be arranged in a descending order of the required criteria. If a mix of boys and girls is required, ensure that the sexes alternate or form two lines for numbering.

Teams can be arranged using braids. A class of 24 has to be arranged into 3 groups of 8. Select eight braids of 3 different colours. Scatter on floor. Class running in hall; on command each gets a braid, puts it on and sits down — 3 groups of 8.

Grouping can be part of the lesson. For example, groups of 3 are needed for the 'Something new section'. The last item of the introductory part can be free running with dodging but on call of a number pupils quickly form groups of that number and sit down. Several calls can be made before you end with the call of '3'. Class now sitting in groups of 3 ready for the next part of the lesson.

A quick way of getting into groups of two is simply to number pupils 1 or 2, A or B. The teacher can call 'Find a partner with the same letter'.

During the 1980s a number of schools considered equal opportunities in relation to gender and promptly mixed all classes for all activities. By the mid 1990s it was reported that such policies had in fact exacerbated the problem of differentiation (OFSTED, 1995, p. 4, para 6). Gender is not necessarily an appropriate characteristic to group pupils and should only be used when carefully considered; for example, some schools keep pupils in mixed gender groups for indoor activities (gymnastics and dance) and not for outdoor activities (games, in particular invasion games). Why? Some say that mixing boys and girls for games such as netball and hockey can disadvantage pupils. But is gender an appropriate criterion to use — are all boys good footballers? are all girls poor footballers?

Organising resources

Part 5 provides a detailed discussion on the management of PE resources within the school. However it is appropriate here to examine how the organisation of resources can play a significant part in creating an effective learning environment (OFSTED, 1993, p. 6). PE makes use of a variety of equipment which is used indoors and outdoors. Teachers have a responsibility to ensure that they are familiar with equipment use, storage and maintenance, and use efficient organisation strategies in their lessons. Furthermore they have to teach children how to accept responsibility for the safe use of equipment at all times.

Instructions and communication

One of the teacher's most valuable resources is the ability to communicate with pupils. This relies on the voice, the ability to offer clear and concise instructions. But remember:

DO	keep it simple	DO NOT	overload
	keep it brief		talk too much
	be enthusiastic		openly criticise effort
	be sure every one is listening		
	inject expression into the voice		

Demonstration is perhaps one of the teacher's most effective teaching aids as it offers an essential visual dimension to the teaching and learning process. 'Modelling' helps create an image for the learner and is seen as an important part of the early stages of motor skill learning (Pollock and Lee, 1992). To make the most of demonstrations encourage teachers to think about:

Positioning — can every one see?

Can the pupils see what they are *supposed to see*? It is not unusual for pupils to be standing in front of a pupil demonstrating a tennis serve when they are supposed to be looking at the over-arm action.

Whole demonstration allows pupils to form a mental picture of the complete activity before focusing on a specific part.

Speed — occasionally demonstrations are performed at normal speed and are over before pupils have had the chance to focus. If the performance is slowed down it would provide time to look and actually see.

Cues — if demonstrations are to be successful teaching aids then pupils need to know what to look for. Cues help focus pupils attention.

Many teachers will ask 'What if I can't demonstrate the things I am asking the pupils to do?' A simple answer is 'You don't have to'. Teachers need only demonstrate the things which they feel comfortable doing. In most instances there will be pupils in your class who can demonstrate for you. This is an important resource that teachers can use, particularly as children like to demonstrate and like to see their peers demonstrating. However, it is important that a variety of children are used. The teacher should focus the demonstrations by describing or questioning:

Which hand is Abigail using to bounce the ball?

Let's watch Rebecca's sequence and see how she links the rolls together.

Watch Gareth moving through the water — but only watch his head. How does he breathe?

Can you see how my arm is bent and it is supposed to be. . . . ?

On a smaller scale, using partners is excellent for close observation skills, for example:

Kate, watch Alexander's hands or feet, can you comment on what you have seen?

Teachers who do not feel able to demonstrate can turn this into a learning situation by acknowledging their limitations. Discussions with pupils can help point out the differences between people and that not everyone will be able to do everything at the same time and all of the time! This sharing can help develop a cooperative learning environment where individual strengths and difficulties are recognised. It is important to address the issue of 'failure' and that learning is not always instant. It can and will involve dealing with failure — it is part of the process of learning.

Positioning of the teacher is central to his or her interaction with the class. Teacher–pupil interaction is ongoing and constant throughout all lessons, be it through verbal or visual communication. The teacher must be aware of all pupils and have a clear view of the class at all times. Encourage your colleagues to think about: Where should the teacher stand to get an overall position? How do different activities influence the teacher's position, e.g. in a gymnasium full of equipment? on the playground? in the swimming pool? when children are in the changing rooms? What happens if the teacher is called away? Your school's policy on safe practice should address this aspect of a teacher's role.

Feedback

Children like and need praise and feedback, and there is no doubt that knowledgeable feedback can benefit performance. It can either give specific information to help correct a faulty response or just sufficient information to enable the learner to make a decision on improving the response. For teachers to make good use of feedback they need to be knowledgeable about the mechanics of movement, be aware of major cues and be able to analyse an action and determine why/where it may have gone wrong. Gaps in subject knowledge therefore have to be identified and built into INSET courses for colleagues.

Tattersfield (1985) summarises the research into the values and effects of augmented feedback and suggests:

> Feedback should be supplied as soon as possible after a skill has taken place, further attempt should then take place.
> This further attempt should preferably be before there has been any intervening activity.
> The longer feedback is delayed the less value it generally has.
> Feedback should be related to an individual's performance. 'Blanket' comments are of limited value.
> The amount of frequency of augmented feedback should be gradually reduced in order to avoid over-dependence on the teacher.
> Even high level performers occasionally require augmented feedback.

Differentiation in PE

A positive learning environment is one where all pupils are motivated to learn. According to Good and Brophy (1991) this needs three conditions:

> A supportive learning environment in which the teacher is patient and encourages pupils' efforts;
> A task is clear, at an appropriate level of difficulty and in which they might achieve high levels of success with reasonable effort;
> A task that is challenging, interesting, meaningful, and worthwhile, such that pupils can see the reasons for learning the activity.

All this relies on teachers 'understanding' their pupils and being able to provide differentiated tasks. Differentiation is probably the most *challenging* aspect of any teacher's work:

'Teaching is more than Instructing. Instructing is one aspect of teaching. It is the single aspect, however, that the general public considers to be the total process of teaching. A teacher who is clever and witty is often considered to be effective. What experienced teachers know is that the real measure of success as a teacher is what the children are doing — and how they feel about what they are doing–that makes the difference. Motivating children to work hard and continue to practice requires much more than simply providing a clever set of instructions.' (Graham, 1992, p. 65)

> *... even in these good lessons, some teachers were more able than others to plan for differentiation of learning according to ability, by both task and outcome. Even able teachers too often resorted to setting tasks and practices which neglected the needs of both ends of the ability range within their classes.*
>
> (OFSTED, 1995, p. 4, para 6)

This challenge must not be underestimated, particularly when teachers may have limited subject knowledge, a lack of confidence, class sizes of 24 if not 30 plus pupils, and limited equipment — to name just a few issues. If teachers are to provide an entitlement curriculum for all pupils, then it is important that differentiated learning is planned.

There are many forms of differentiation available to the teacher, outlined below.

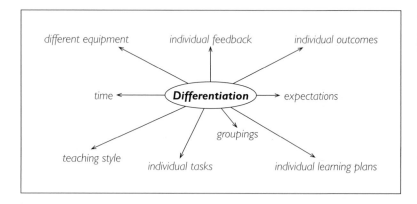

These various forms offer different levels of differentiation and will be suitable for teachers with varying amounts of experience. For example, it is unreasonable to expect the newly qualified teacher to offer lessons accommodating individual learning plans. A starting point would be for the NQT to focus on the upper part of the figure and aim at individual interpretations of a common task, thus differentiating by outcome. Or a whole class task could be presented in such an open-ended way that pupils would be able to work at their own level. Or pupils could choose types of equipment suitable to their needs. Or the teacher could offer pupils individual feedback. More experienced teachers should work towards catering for individuals when planning tasks and lessons: preparation would involve designing individual tasks with individual expectations. It is important to remember that

Suggestion

Select a learning objective from a lesson plan or unit of work. Describe how the teacher can explicitly provide for pupil involvement.
Chose a task from a particular activity area. How is differentiation achieved?
What are the different expectations of two pupils for the same task?

Suggestion

Reflect on a specific lesson and choose a task. This may be done using video materials. Did all pupils complete the task? Was it challenging? Does the task need modifying? How? Why? In order to achieve what?

different styles of teaching are more appropriate for differentiation than others; for example, those focusing on problem solving, guided discovery and inclusion can all promote individual learning plans, and encourage children to work independently and accommodate different needs.

Monitoring and evaluating

Managing effective teaching and learning involves *monitoring and evaluating* what is actually going on in lessons. NEELB use the framework in Figure 5.3 to evaluate the quality of teaching.

FIG 5.3
A framework for evaluating the quality of teaching

The quality of teaching in physical education is good when:
- there is clear evidence the lesson is part of a unit of work which takes full account of the Programmes of Study and the End of Key Stage Descriptors;
- learning objectives and assessment criteria for the lessons and units are clearly identified by the teacher and shared with pupils;
- the learning environment is safe and secure for all pupils;
- pupils progress safely and with good pace from one task to the next;
- the content is appropriate to the age, ability and physical development of the pupils;
- a range of grouping strategies enables all pupils to participate fully and experience success and enjoyment;
- time is used efficiently, appropriately and effectively;
- the activities are physically and intellectually demanding, expectations and challenges are high but obtainable;
- opportunities are provided for all pupils to display knowledge and understanding of health-related issues;
- an appropriate range of teaching styles enables pupils to:
  - plan, perform and evaluate their own and others' activity;
  - solve problems, answer questions and learn techniques which match their age and ability;
  - consolidate and refine through practise and repetition;
  - demonstrate knowledge and understanding;
  - observe and feedback on performance;
  - work alone, in pairs and in groups;
  - progress to independent learning;
  - use a range of equipment and resources;
- assessment and discussion of work is positive, effective and motivating;
- relationships between adults and pupils and within peer groups are positive;
- non-participation make clear and purposeful contributions to the lesson in terms of planning and evaluation.

(*Source*: NEELB Guidance)

The following questionnaires and proformas are designed to help you evaluate the quality of teaching and learning in PE in your school. However, remember to consider *why* you are evaluating teaching and learning, the *means* of recording evidence and *who* has access to any reports.

Identifying the key principle of teaching and learning

This could serve as a summary sheet to conclude a whole school discussion:

Avondale School — Staff Development Day
Wednesday 21 June 1997
QUALITY OF TEACHING AND LEARNING

Q. What do you consider to be the essential characteristics of quality and teaching and learning in physical education?

Focusing on a specific aspect of good teaching in gymnastics

This questionnaire could be used with different groups of teachers.

Woodstock Primary School — Staff Development Day
QUALITY OF TEACHING AND LEARNING IN GYMNASTICS

The focus of the session is to watch four short sequences of teachers taking gymnastics lessons.

While watching these sequences consider the following points with regard to quality of teaching and learning:

(a) With regard to teaching and learning, which sequence impressed you most?

(b) Why did it impress you most?

(c) What points with regard to teaching, impressed you?

(d) Did the children appear to be learning?

(e) Which sequence with regard to teaching and learning, did you like least and why?

(f) Can you identify good teaching points from all four sequences?

(g) Can you identify some bad points with regard to the teaching?

Alternatively you could focus on:

■ different teaching methods;
■ different learning activities;
■ specific aspects of organisation;
■ a general approach using an open recording proforma for any PE activity.

You may find the following questionnaires helpful when evaluating teaching and learning in your school.

DIFFERENT TEACHING METHODS — WHAT DO YOU USE?

TEACHING STRATEGY	How Often	Learning objective	Which activity
Organisation: whole group			
small group			
partner work			
Problem-solving			
Differentiation: tasks			
outcomes			
equipment			
expectations			
Demonstrations: pupil			
teacher			
Assessment: pupil self-assessment			
peer assessment			
Resources			
Task cards/checklists			
Circuits			
Cross-curricular/themes/projects			

(*Source*: NEELB Guidance)

MONITORING DIFFERENT LEARNING ACTIVITIES — WHAT DO PUPILS EXPERIENCE?			
LEARNING ACTIVITY	**How Often**	**Learning objective**	**Which activity**
Listening and observing			
Demonstrating			
Decision making			
Questioning			
Planning/composing			
Evaluating/judging			
Adapting/refining			
Communicating			
Recording			
Cooperating			
Sharing			
Measuring			
Matching			
Persuading			
Describing			
Remembering			

(*Source*: adapted from Hereford and Worcester Curriculum Guidelines 1992)

SELF-ASSESSMENT — Cranfield School

When reviewing your lesson it is helpful to ask yourself some basic questions. The following is a suggested list. Some of the questions will need adapting according to the type of class being taught.

ADMINISTRATION: YES   NO

1. Was my lesson well prepared?

2. Was the lesson punctual in starting?

3. Were the children suitably dressed for the activity?

4. Did they have proper footwear for the activity?

5. Was I suitably dressed?

6. Did I collect dangerous articles, e.g. watches and rings etc.?

7. Was the apparatus required for immediate use readily available?

8. Was the apparatus required distributed around the room?

9. Did my class replace the apparatus carefully and safely, so that the next class found it in good order?

10. Did I finish on time to allow a safe and orderly finish and so that the next class was not delayed?

OFSTED criteria is useful for lesson observation and is shown in Figure 5.4.

Whatever methods of evaluation or 'audit' you use, be sure to align it with the aims and objectives of your PE programme and more importantly, be sure everyone is aware of it.

Content of the Observation

- brief summary of lesson content, activities and organisation.
- brief description of role of any support and/or adult present.
- interview (include time)

TEACHING   **Evidence and Evaluation**

Does the teacher:

- have a secure knowledge and understanding of the subject or area being taught?
- set high expectations so as to challenge pupils and deepen their knowledge and understanding?
- plan effectively?
- employ methods and organisational strategies which match curricular objectives and the needs of all pupils?
- manage pupils well and achieve high standards of discipline?
- use time and resources effectively?
- assess pupils' work thoroughly and constructively and use assessments to inform teaching?
- use homework effectively to reinforce and/or extend what is learnt in schools?

RESPONSE (attitudes)

Do all the pupils present:

- show involvement, enjoyment and application?
- work independently to generate ideas and solve problems?
- show pride in their financed work?
- work collaboratively when required?
- show initiative and willingness to take responsibility?
- sustain and respond to challenge?
- persevere and complete task when difficulties arise?
- form constructive relationships with one another, and with the teacher?
- show respect for each other's views and work?

ATTAINMENT

Assess what pupils know, understand and can do in this subject.

This is an age-related judgement which should *not* make allowance for pupils' perceived potential or ability.

How does the attainment of all pupils:

- compare *either* with national averages in terms of results in key stages, assessments and external examinations *or* to national expectations.
- highlight relative strengths and weaknesses across different aspects of the subject and also significant variations in attainment among different groups of pupils e.g. more and less able.

PROGRESS (Gains in knowledge, understanding and skills in this subject)

- are pupils consolidating previous learning?
- is there evidence of new learning taking place?
- do high, average and low attainment pupils, including those with SEN, progress as well or better than expected?
- is the progress of minority groups comparable with others in the school?
- is there evidence of information seeking, posing questions, solving problems, modes of communicating information and ideas?

Other significant evidence

Make notes on SEN, EO, ARR and key skills-Writing, Reading, S & L, IT and Number Effect of Resourcing/Accommodation/class size.

Grades: Excellent, 2 Very good, 3 Good, 4 Satisfactory, 5 Unsatisfactory, 6 Poor, 7 Very poor.

FIG 5.4
Sample Observation Form, OFSTED 1996

Chapter 6

Developing a framework for safe practice

As coordinator you will inevitably have a responsibility for ensuring that a **safe learning environment is provided for all pupils**. Whilst this relates very much to the principles discussed in earlier chapters, there are specific issues which involve:

■ knowing what safe practice means;
■ establishing responsibilities;
■ understanding why accidents happen and knowing how to prevent them;
■ securing working policies.

The TTA (1996) have included such a responsibility in their proposed qualification for subject leaders, stating

> ❝ *Subject leaders will be expected to have knowledge and understanding of . . . health and safety requirements.* (p. 10)

There is little description of what this exactly means, but more specific responsibilities will be evident from the detailed job description agreed by you with the headteacher.

This chapter will address some of the key issues about responsibility and offer guidance on how to secure a safe environment for both teachers and pupils in your school.

What is safe practice?

Safe practice means that teachers and others in positions of responsibility have *a duty of care* for those in their charge. This involves the recognition of safety as an important element in their work (BAALPE, 1995, p. 7). Physical education, by its very nature, has an element of **risk** and **challenge**, so providing a safe environment does not mean that teachers remove the risk involved. It means that teachers have to ensure they are *aware* of the risks and that the young people in their care are properly prepared to manage these risks and develop the skills necessary to ensure their own and others' safety. This approach towards safe practice must be 'whole school' and be explicit in all curriculum materials and monitored in practice.

Within schools, some subjects and activities, more than others, offer the potential for accident and hazard. The possibility of risk and accident is recognised to be greater in practical school subjects, and physical education is recognised as a high risk area (Croner, 1987). Along with others I would argue that there is risk in almost everything we do and that safety cannot be guaranteed or ensured because unforeseen conditions, improper decisions and poor judgment can all generate risk or hazard. Despite close management, organisation and supervision of pupils, schools, like other social environments, are susceptible to accident or risk, so it is important that teachers and all those responsible for children are reminded that they must operate within the appropriate legal framework.

Athletics, dance, gymnastics, games, outdoor and adventurous activities and swimming combine to form a broad and balanced range of experiences in physical education. Each of these areas will also involve challenge and adventure. This is not to say they are dangerous, but teachers need to be fully conscious of their professional duty to ensure a safe learning environment and to be concerned with minimising the risks. However, providing a safe environment is not the sole responsibility of teachers — central government, national associations, local education authorities (LEAs), school governing bodies, and you as subject coordinator, along with other individual colleagues all play a part in what must be seen as a collective responsibility.

Areas of responsibility

The different areas of responsibility have been identified as legal, professional and moral (Raymond and Thomas, 1996).

Legal responsibilities

The law now expects that all physical education teachers will work within a 'modus operandi' which identifies all the foreseeable safety problems associated with the activities undertaken in relation to the school curriculum.

> *Common Law and statute law impose general duties on individuals and bodies. Any breach of these duties which causes injury or loss may give rise to a claim for damages (compensation), or sometimes even to criminal penalties. Although accidents will occur because they cannot always be foreseen, teachers have a legal duty to work within a system which demonstrates a realistic use of methods which successfully anticipate and eliminate foreseeable risks.* (BAALPE, 1995, p. 21)

The legal responsibilities are stipulated in a number of documents, including the Health and Safety at Work Act 1974 (HSW Act). This Act requires that employers (local authorities, governing bodies, managers of other premises including outdoor centres) and the self-employed are legally required to do all that is reasonably practicable to ensure the health and safety of employees (teachers, instructors, coaches and all other staff) and non-employees (pupils and others who enter the premises, e.g. parents) who are affected by their undertaking.

Section 2(3) of the HSW Act places a *duty of care* on every employer (LEA) to prepare, and as often as appropriate to revise, a written statement on general policy in respect of the health and safety at work of employees and the organisation and arrangements for the time being in force for carrying out that policy. The employer must also bring the statement and any revision of it to the notice of employees (teachers). This also applies to safe premises and safe environment in which employees and pupils will work. This is an important area particularly when working off-site, external to the school or when involved with activities where circumstances can change rapidly.

The standard of care required of teachers is that 'which from an objective point of view can reasonably be expected from teachers generally applying skill and awareness of children's problems, needs and susceptibilities' (NUT, 1992, p. 4).

As well as the HSW Act, the Management of Health and Safety at Work 1992 regulations set down the revised guidelines that require employers to introduce measures for planning, organising, monitoring and reviewing their arrangements for the management of health and safety: Risk Assessment. These most recent guidelines required governing bodies and their headteachers to, first, identify and assess the levels of risk that exist in curriculum activities and, second, to ensure the design and implementation of effective risk control measures, appropriate systems, procedures and policies to manage, control and protect these measures and to develop through adequate health and safety training.

Additionally, teachers operate within the framework of 'common law', where there are long-established and important requirements for those acting in *loco parentis*. This forms the basis for duty of care which applies both to the school curriculum and extra-curricular activities, whether undertaken on or away from the school premises. When involved in school trips, residential type experiences etc. duty of care is twenty-four hours a day.

> *Teachers and others with this legal responsibility must exercise the same duty of care as would a reasonable parent. In the case of pupils on adventurous activities, or at recreational and sports centres, this legal responsibility falls to the accompanying teachers and cannot be delegated to instructors or coaches.*
>
> (BAALPE, 1995, p. 22)

It is worth nothing that both parents and the general public often set the professional responsibility for children's well-being and safety much higher than that normally expected of a parent: they presume that teachers will be *more* aware of the potential dangers to pupils. It is up to the coordinator to keep colleagues aware of what is considered to be acceptable practice.

Professional responsibilities

In England and Wales a teacher's professional duties are set out in the *School Teachers Pay and Conditions Document* which is published annually. An important paragraph includes

> *... maintaining good order and discipline among the pupils and safeguarding their health and safety both when they are authorized to be on the school premises and when they are engaged in authorized school activities elsewhere.* (1995, par. 35)

The coordinator's role, then is to:
- Help teachers keep up to date and aware of these Conditions. This will help ensure that teachers are in a position to identify and analyse the risks involved in the school curriculum activities and subsequently develop and implement strategies and policies to manage such risk and minimise the possibility of accident and injury. The thinking behind policy-making should be reflected in the curriculum guidelines and evident by the choice of activities and equipment to be used by different groups.
- Raise teachers' awareness of regular and approved practice in PE.
- Make available evidence to illustrate that a reasonable standard of care in terms of planning, organisation and delivery has been provided.

Moral responsibilities

There is a fine line between those responsibilities considered professional and those which may be considered of a moral nature. The latter refers to a teacher's responsibility to ensure that pupils do not feel unreasonably pressurised, or coerced to attempt activities where their anxiety or fear might contribute to an emotionally unrewarding experience or failure to participate safely.

Why do accidents happen?

The initial stage in securing a framework for safe practice is to be aware of and understand the teacher's legal, professional and moral responsibilities. Some colleagues have little awareness of the responsibilities they hold and are unaware of the rapid increase in legal action against schools and LEAs. With this in mind, you could raise their awareness by looking at case studies of accidents that have happened and asking why these happened — there is much to be learnt from others.

Despite differences in pupils' age, the type of school, range of setting and activity type, Thomas (1994) considers there are similarities as to *why* accidents happen. She suggests five elements:

Bad luck — factors outside the teachers' control.
Poor decision-making and subsequent reaction to the situation.
Lack of adequate and appropriate group management, supervision and organisation.
The over-estimation of (a) teacher's ability (knowledge, understanding and competence);
(b) the pupil's sense of responsibility.
The under-estimation of potential risk and hazard.

So, apart from the element of 'bad luck' there is much that teachers can do avoid accidents and much to explain why an accident is not an 'incident'.

Managing safe practice

There are various approaches to the management of safe practice, the following are most commonly found in educational settings: *risk management* and *negligence avoidance.*

Risk management

Risk management requires a careful evaluation of what could happen to pupils, teachers or others in the teaching and learning environment. The National Association of Independent Schools (1988) describe it as a formal process of assessing exposure to risk and taking whatever action is necessary to minimise its impact. Under the *Management of Health and Safety at Work* regulations (1992) **risk assessment** is a legal requirement and it is the responsibility of the governors and headteacher to ensure that risk assessment is carried out. BAALPE (1995) recommend that risk assessment should be applied wherever foreseeable risks or hazards may occur. They describe a hazard as 'anything that may cause harm' while a risk is 'the chance that someone may be harmed by the hazard' (p. 43). Others see the management of risk as a series of processes:

- recognising and identifying the presence of risk;
- evaluating and assessing the potential degree (real or apparent, physical or emotional);
- judging the appropriateness of the risk in relation to intended learning objectives and outcomes;
- harnessing the risk within the learning activities selected through appropriate teaching styles, presentation of opportunities and learning environment;
- being able to cope with the planned and unplanned outcomes of classroom activity. This involves the skills of adaptability and forseeability. (Raymond and Thomas, 1996, p. 30)

These processes are largely common sense and logical, but that is not to demean their importance. Risk management is the responsibility of all teachers, as risk managers, and they must decide whether a hazard is significant and, if so, to determine and implement the precautions or actions necessary to eliminate or minimise the risks presented.

Pupils must also be encouraged to take responsibility for their own safety. This is explicit in the National Curriculum general requirements.

To ensure safe practice, pupils should be taught:
! to respond readily to instructions;
! to recognise and follow relevant rules, laws, codes, etiquette and safety procedures for different activities or events, in practise and during competition;
! about the safety risks of wearing inappropriate clothing, footwear and jewellery, and why particular clothing, footwear and protection are worn for different activities;
! how to lift, carry, place and use equipment safely;
! to warm up for and recover from exercise.   (DfE, 1995, p. 2)

When designing a PE programme, teachers must consider the risks involved in different activities. When delivering lesson materials teachers must refer to this information and select appropriate learning opportunities. Recommended practice requires that teachers:

- consider the total event or activity before it takes place, break this down into phases and then assess each phase for its hazards and risks. *What potential hazards can be reasonably foreseen?*
- having identified these, think of the precautions needed and take steps to ensure that these are implemented. *Is the risk controlled for each foreseeable hazard? Is further action necessary?*
- share the process with other adults involved in the activity and the ensuing information with all participants.
  (BAAPLE, 1995, p. 43)

Records of risk assessment and any discussions should be formally recorded and kept as an evidence base that the check took place. At regular intervals the PE coordinator should review the activity and take note of experiences and of any particular hazard or risk which should additionally be revised during risk management. An obvious need for risk assessment is in the planning and organisation of journeys and visits, but it must also apply to aspects of the PE programme where hazards are apparent; for example, gymnastics, and swimming. The process of risk management is therefore an integral part of schemes of work, programmes of study, units and lesson planning. Wherever possible all colleagues should be involved in the process.

Negligence avoidance

The second approach to the management of safe practice is negligence avoidance. This involves teachers in many of the same processes identified under risk management; the fundamental difference is that the teacher's primary concern here is with the prevention of litigation and the 'protection' of the self, local education authority and the school. This approach to PE may change some features of the PE programme, because:

Think about

As PE coordinator you will clearly have responsibility for creating and monitoring safe practice.

Do you have a PE safety policy?

Are you and your colleagues aware of the responsibilities relating to 'duty of care'?

- Teachers should think of pupils and parents as potential claimants and adversaries.
- There may be reduced curricular and extra-curricular activities and opportunities because the perceived risk of legal action is seen to outweigh the educational benefit.
- There may be an increase in (safer) traditional teaching methods involving didactic and command style teaching and inflexible organisational strategies.

As British and European society becomes more aware of legal rights and issues of entitlement, and cases of litigation increase, so negligence avoidance is rapidly becoming the dominant approach (Laurence, 1988; Gray, 1995).

These two approaches clearly impact upon the curriculum in different ways. Securing a safe environment is not a case of either/or, but involves a synthesis of strategies.

The threat of legal action is both traumatic and damaging for the school, teacher and the pupil. It can also be costly. We should all be aware of the need for preventative action. In 'A cautionary tale of negligence' Bramwell (1993) contends that it is the responsibility of the management team of any school to protect their staff by constructing the necessary defences. He suggests that after an incident certain questions will be asked to ascertain if the school was negligent and offers the following checklist:

1 Could the accident have been prevented? In other words, was the accident reasonably foreseeable?
2 Was the activity undertaken, and the equipment being used, appropriate to the age and experience of the children?
3 Were the children given adequate warnings about the dangers of misusing equipment?
4 Did the organisation of the lesson follow normal and accepted practice?
5 Did the teacher involved stick to school? LEA policy?
6 Did the child receive swift and effective attention after the incident? (Bramwell, 1993, p. 32)

It is important that your school develops a tighter emphasis on systems and procedures to manage and control health and safety risks. As coordinator it will be for you to involve colleagues in the ongoing development of such policies and strategies. It is also worth remembering that schools are just one of the many partners involved in education, and responsibility for safe practice in PE also lies with advisers, inspectors and teacher educators. You should place particular emphasis on establishing:

■ **Policies and Practice**

What are the school/subject safety policies?

How are these reflected in the curriculum guidelines which specify the activities and equipment to be used by various groups?

Are the policies, including all procedures and routines readily available? Are they circulated to all staff including student-teachers, supply teachers and sports coaches working in partnership.

Insurance — The PE coordinator and the headteacher should ensure that there is adequate insurance cover for PE and school sporting activities. This can be done through your LEA, the PE adviser or an independent insurance broker. Check your school's legal liability cover. Are all school colleagues and teaching assistants members of a union or professional association?

Care and maintenance of facilities and equipment — Who regularly checks PE 'classrooms' and teaching resources? Is there procedure for recording breakages, repairs, etc.? When are checks undertaken? (This is dealt with in further detail in Part 5.)

Volunteer helpers — Are they aware of their responsibilities to provide a duty of care? Who is responsible for checking that helpers have the relevant knowledge and awareness of safety issues? Who monitors the quality of experience that children receive? The Children Act, which received Royal assent in 1989 and came into force in October 1991, charges local authorities with two main duties: (i) they must hold a register of all activities for children under the age of 8; (ii) they must ensure activities and services are provided that ensure the health and development of all children, and this includes the use of suitably qualified staff.

■ **Curriculum Planning**

Detailed documents outlining the PE curriculum, programmes of study, units of work, etc. offer a good evidence base should there be an accident and legal investigation into negligence. They should not only reflect the quality of learning provided for pupils but address issues of progression and safe practice throughout the whole curriculum. Is the school curriculum appropriate for your classes? Do you meet the legal requirements? Are tasks suitable for all pupils?

■ **Staff Development**

Teachers should receive relevant inservice training to keep them up-to-date with information of current issues and changes. Case studies of negligence may be used to raise understanding and awareness of the 'duty of care' and illustrate specific dangers and aspects of responsibility.

Schools working in Initial Teacher Training Partnership also have a 'duty of care' to student-teachers. When student-teachers are placed in your school, the headteacher will have agreed to a legally binding contract with a higher education institution and will be responsible for providing a formal training programme. When student-teachers teach PE it is important that they work alongside their mentor teachers: they must not be left on their own, as clearly stated in the BAALPE (1995) guidance:

❝ *Students on teaching practice should always be supervised by qualified teachers. Even though they may reasonably assume greater responsibility for classes as their initial teacher training progresses, it is important to realise they cannot assume full in loco parentis responsibility until they are finally qualified on satisfactory completion of their courses. This responsibility is retained by the class teachers and cannot be transferred.* (p. 33)

How much do you know?

The following scenarios will enable you to think about how much you know about safe practice.

Gymnastics — facilities

All Key Stage 2 pupils will engage in a Programme of Study for gymnastics. On average there are 28 pupils in each class, lessons are taught in the school hall and each class will make use of the gymnastics equipment. Before considering the actual activities that pupils will engage in

Consider the environment. What risks are involved in using the school hall and equipment? How will you make use of the school hall and equipment?

Consider the hall:

- FLOOR — Is this clean and dust free? Is it slippery? Are there any wet patches from roof leaks or condensation? Are there any loose wooden boards, splintering, cracking or irregular surfaces which may cause damage?
- LIGHTING — Are there any concerns about the quality of light for pupils working? Are lights protected or the units made of unbreakable materials? Is there any danger that strip-lighting will produce a flickering or stroboscopic effect and thus cause visual disorientation?
- WALLS — Are these in good repair with obstacles out of reach? Are there any looped ropes hanging?
- DOORS — Glass doors are hazardous: Are they reinforced and resistant to impact fracture? Do they have a system of closure control to avoid unexpected slamming?
- HEATING AND VENTILATION — Are children working in an adequate temperature? Is there adequate circulation of air? Are systems regularly checked and maintained?
- FIRE EXITS — Are these clearly marked and does everyone know the procedure in case of fire? How often is a fire drill experienced when a class are working in the hall? As coordinator you may be involved in organising such drills.

Now consider the apparatus, both portable and fixed:

- INSPECTION — When did you last inspect the equipment for wear and tear? Is this a regular procedure? Do you have a certificate for 'safe usage'? What happens once your hall has been inspected? Is there a system of daily/weekly monitoring?
- STORAGE AND MANAGEMENT — Do arrangements ensure that equipment is secure and away from easy interference of pupils? Can pupils easily access equipment when required? Are warning signs and instructions clearly visible? Are instructions clear for pupils and staff?
- HANDLING EQUIPMENT — Do all teachers know how to handle equipment and how to teach pupils to safely handle equipment, according to their age and strength? Are there agreed policies involving correct procedures, rules and regulations for children handling and working with the equipment?

Gymnastics — Content and the use of progressions
A class of 28, Year 6 pupils are timetabled for gymnastics. The focus of the floor-work part of the lesson is transference of weight involving inversion: this could involve all pupils performing shoulder stands, and some or all pupils performing headstands and handstands.

What risks are involved in these activities?

- STYLE OF TEACHING — Which styles of teaching are most appropriate and why?
- TASKS — How can you engage pupils in activities involving turning upside down, balancing and then coming back to their feet safely? What are the most appropriate progressions for pupils to learn the skills?
- TEACHER SUPPORTING — Do you know acceptable supporting techniques? Can you support children of varying size with confidence?
- CHILDREN SUPPORTING EACH OTHER — Are pupils clear about the role of supporting? Are they capable? Have they been taught how to support correctly?
- CHILDREN'S ABILITY — Do you know the pupils involved in the activity? Are they all capable of performing all or just some of the skills? Who may lack confidence? Who may have too much confidence? Are colleagues aware of DFEE circular 10/95 'Protecting Children from Abuse: The Role of the Education Service'?
- CLASS MANAGEMENT — How will you organise the children in the gym/hall? Will they be in friendship groups, ability groups, gender groups?
- ORGANISATION OF EQUIPMENT — What equipment will you need? How will this be organised in the hall? How will the children take out and put away the equipment? Will children use mats? Why?

Swimming — Travel to the pool

A Year 5 class of 28 pupils using the local swimming pool. Pupils have to walk about 500 metres to the local university pool.
What risks are involved?

- TRAVEL BETWEEN THE TWO SITES — Who will supervise the pupils? Is the staff–pupil ratio acceptable? Are there pathways along the route? Will children have to cross any main or side roads? What are the agreed procedures of good practice?
- CHANGING FACILITIES — Are these appropriate and free from any danger? What happens to children's personal belongings?
- SWIMMING POOL — Does the pool meet the requirements of the code of practice as recommended by the Health and Safety Executive for public swimming pools? Is the log book outlining pool temperatures, chlorine levels, etc., easily available to staff for checking? Are there adequate life saving procedures? Are water depths clearly displayed? Are hygiene and safety standards acceptable? Where does the duty of care reside when you are using outside pools? Are emergency procedures clear and are all users aware of them?

- PUPILS — Do pupils know the accepted code of good conduct? Do pupils know what to do in case of an accident or emergency? Do pupils take care with their hygiene? Do they know their own limitations?
- PUPILS AND TEACHERS — Do teachers know the limitations of their pupils? Are they aware of special needs, any ailments, worries etc.? Is good use made of resources, particularly buoyancy aids. Are there acceptable procedures in place for good conduct?
- SUPERVISION — What is the teacher–pupil ratio? Is this acceptable? Can you see all the pupils throughout the lesson? Are pupils registered or counted at the beginning and end of each lesson? Is the supervisor in the pool qualified?

Games — netball
A Year 4 class following an invasion games unit, 28 pupils. The unit is focusing on netball.
What risks are involved?
- PLAYGROUND — Is the tarmac in good repair? Are there any uneven patches/drains?
- POSTS — Are these secure and well balanced?
- COURT MARKINGS — Do the outside boundary lines leave space for movement around the court away from windows, walls and spectators?
- SURROUNDING NETTING — Is this in good repair?
- WEATHER — Are conditions comfortable for safe play? Temperature? Rain/frost?
- CHILDREN'S KIT — Are pupils wearing sutiable footwear? Have they removed jewellery and dangerous objects?

This chapter clearly carries a HEALTH WARNING, it may generate some anxiety but it is important that you know the extent of your responsibility for safety in a subject which has 'risk' and 'challenge' as an essential ingredient. Safety and the curriculum is clearly receiving a much higher profile in the minds of all those concerned about the welfare of both teachers and children. School staff and pupils must work together to promote safe learning.

Such an in-depth look at these activities may put some colleagues off as they could be seen as too much work — even over the top! But risk management should be part of our daily work, and it takes time. If any of this is left to chance then you could not only be putting children at risk, but teachers and schools.

Part three

Whole school policies and schemes of work

Chapter 7

Planning a whole school policy for physical education

Paperwork, and keeping it up to date, is often seen as one of the most onerous tasks for teachers. Some teachers think there is too much of it, but in today's climate of accountability there is little choice, at least not without penalty! Accepting responsibility for 'paperwork' is the first step, next you have to find out what exactly you have to do, get it done, and keep it up to date using simple, efficient methods. All of this will take time, consultation and discussion along with coping with the reality and day-to-day pressures of daily school life.

Planning and the quality of teaching

PE documents reflect the school's curriculum and outline the progressive and continuous experiences for pupils. Good planning is a means to achieving this and is recognised as a prerequisite for effective teaching. Teacher planning and preparation is very much a process in which, according to Clark and Peterson (1986), teachers visualise the future, devise goals, implement methods and procedures, and construct frameworks for future action. Having subject knowledge is not enough, the teacher needs to have pedagogical knowledge about the principles of teaching and learning (see Part Two, Chapter 5; Wilson et al., 1987; Schulman, 1987; Mawer, 1995). This embraces knowledge of the learner, of previous learning experiences, of the curriculum, of the school context, of different teaching styles, and techniques of class management. As Mawer (1995) summarises:

❝ *Planning appears to mediate between a teacher's basic knowledge of the subject being taught and his or her ability to teach the subject effectively.*

(p. 55)

Several researchers (Peterson and Clark, 1978; Imwold et al., 1984; Clark and Yinger, 1987; Griffey and Housner, 1991; Byra and Coulon, 1994) have investigated various aspects of planning and its effects on teacher behaviour and effectiveness during lessons. The results of such research over two decades clearly identify that planning improves the quality of teaching and learning; it focuses learning, pupils are more actively involved, and it helps teachers make more effective use of equipment, resources and time. In my own small-scale research, undergraduate and postgraduate student-teachers were invited to write about teaching competence and to list what they considered to be the ten most important teaching skills. This task was initially completed before they went out on final teaching placements and planning and preparation emerged as one of the top ten competences, but only featured midway down their list of ten skills. On return from 10 weeks in school, the student-teachers repeated the task and planning, along with subject knowledge, emerged as one of the top two most important competences for effective teaching.

How to plan

So we know planning is essential but how do we do it? Any planning requires background details and knowledge of

- the National Curriculum and specifically each Programme of Study and End of Key Stage Descriptors (EKSD)
- the school context and PE as a subject, time available
- the pupils
- the teachers
- the resources.

All of this preparation must also reflect the principles underpinning the curriculum as discussed in Part Two. It is your responsibility to coordinate a whole school approach to physical education thus ensuring progression, continuity and consistency in provision. Although you will have a major role to play in planning, you cannot be expected to do it all

> Why a school policy? The point of developing a whole school policy is that it is owned by the whole staff, describes what is actually happening on the ground and gives some indication of the direction the school is going with regard to your subject area. (Harrison, 1995, p. 14)

Remember: it is important that policy is driven by teachers and yourself, starting from where you are developing your practice.
It should be collaborative.

on your own. Coordination involves engaging colleagues in discussions, whole school decision making and agreement on the way forward. This promotes a collective approach and should help both you and your colleagues to recognise and work with their strengths and weaknesses.

Good practice also recognises the need for teachers and local advisers to be involved in developing policies and planning schemes together so that they share ideas and collectively make decisions on agreed practice. This can be done through informal conversations or formal discussions and this involvement may actually help their commitment, understanding and classroom practice. However, this sharing of ideas and collective decision making is not easy! Teachers often see you, the coordinator, as responsible for coming up with 'what they have to do', some adopt a 'tell me and I'll do it' attitude and this has to be managed with caution and sensitivity.

There are various stages and levels of planning which require different depths of preparation, each of which needs careful consideration. Here I will consider various stages in curriculum planning needing long-; medium- and short-term plans, and moving from a general overview (whole school) to one that is more specific (individual pupil). All four stages are interdependent and mutually supportive.

1   *Whole school*: How does PE fit into the overall school curriculum? Does it take into account themes and cross-curricular links which permeate all subjects? Is there progression and continuity?
2   *Key Stage*: What skills and processes, knowledge, attitudes are being developed through which activity areas?
3   *Class*: What specific experiences are being used as the focus for planning, performing and evaluating? How will assessment take place?
4   *Individual pupil*: What are the individual needs? How will experiences be differentiated? How will this be managed in the classroom?

An example of how these stages manifest themselves in practice is illustrated by the Devon Curriculum Planning Advice successfully used in schools to develop systematic approaches to planning (see Figure 7.1 p. 140).

FIG 7.1
A model for basic curriculum
planning

AIMS OF THE SCHOOL

SCHOOL DEVELOPMENT PLAN
STAFF DEVELOPMENT PLAN

WHOLE SCHOOL CURRICULUM POLICY
TEACHING AND LEARNING

CURRICULUM POLICIES
PHYSICAL EDUCATION
CROSS-CURRICULAR SKILLS, DIMENSIONS AND THEMES

SCHEMES OF WORK
MAPPING OF SoW/PoS
TIME ALLOCATION FOR UNITS OF WORK

UNITS OF WORK AND ASSESSMENT

INDIVIDUAL LESSONS

CURRICULUM GUIDELINES
NATIONAL CURRICULUM
RESOURCE MANAGEMENT, EQUAL OPPORTUNITIES,
SPECIAL EDUCATIONAL NEEDS, ASSESSMENT, RECORDING
AND REPORTING
HEALTH AND SAFETY

*All aspects of a school's curriculum planning, with the exception of teachers' short
term planning, should be available and accessible to the public, e.g. parents*

(*Source:* adapted from the Devon Curriculum Planning Advice)

What documentation do you need to have available?

It is important that a sensible approach is taken so a sensible answer would be 'Only that which has been written because the school sees it as necessary' (i.e. it is not merely to keep those external to the school happy). There is no standardised format so you will need to consult with the headteacher for guidance on agreed practice. It is not unusual for schools to have their own requirements for all coordinators. Harrison (1995) offers a prototype policy divided into seven sections: Introduction; Implementation; Schemes of work; Assessment of and Recording of Pupils' Progress; Resources; Staff Development; and Review/Evaluation of this Policy. He offers this as a 'skeleton on which to hang your own ideas and suggestions' (p. 15). Throughout this section I will offer further advice on how to put flesh on this skeleton so that the policy offers meaningful detail.

FIG 7.2
PE subject documentation checklist

Do you have the following information readily available?

Introduction
- General organization and management of the subject — infant, junior and secondary liaison staff responsibilities, budget

Policy statement — Implementation
- PE curriculum statement — whole school ethos and rationale
- Teaching and learning (teaching and learning styles, differentiation, progression and continuity)
- Pupils (kit, non-participation, valuables and lost property, rewards and sanctions)
- Assessment, recording and reporting
- Community links — outside agency involvement
- Cross-curricular themes and dimensions
- Equal opportunities, including special needs
- Information Technology
- Initial teacher education (working with student-teachers)
- Resources (equipment, facilities and curriculum materials)
- Health and safety
- Subject evaluation (quality assurance)

Curriculum documentation (including National Curriculum) — Schemes of work
- Aims and objectives
- Assessment, recording and reporting
- Overall syllabus, scheme and Programmes of Study
- Units of work according to activity areas
- Sample lesson material
- Details of community links outside agency involvement

Extra-curricular provision
- Rationale, aims and objectives
- Timetable of clubs
- Details of teams and other school events
- Community links (including use of facilities and expertise)

Subject evaluation and development
- Monitoring procedures
- Annual report
- Staff development and INSET

Suggestion

Examine the PE documentation already in existence at your school.
Identify any areas missing or in need of development.
Outline an action plan, including a possible timetable outlining how the gaps will be filled.

Figures 7.1 and 7.2 are example frameworks and could serve as a useful checklist. At a first glance it can appear quite daunting. How does it compare with your own documentation? Look again and you will begin to see that you already do most, if not all of these things — but they may not all be written down!

Subject planning needs to reflect a message and this should be short, concise and well presented. The following section offers some guidance on developing your policy documents.

> Remember:
> Planning documents evolve over time.

Preparing a PE policy

Compiling a comprehensive set of policy documents will evolve over time, so when preparing your documentation don't expect to get it all done perfectly first time. Someone once gave me some good advice 'don't get it right, get it written'. This means always prepare a first draft, leave it, consult, then redraft with fresh eyes. Consultation means circulating documents to colleagues (all or a selection), asking them for comments, letting them question and challenge it, reshape and hopefully 'own it'. You will also need to consult the headteacher and/or approach another coordinator to review the material. This, plus an annual review, should help to tighten up and improve your material so that eventually you only need to refine detail annually and respond to the latest initiatives.

All physical education policy documents should:
- reflect the school's ethos, its beliefs, values, attitudes and intentions towards the all-round education and development of the child;
- relate to the school development plan.

Whole school curriculum policy statement

What needs to be documented about the physical education curriculum?

Any opening policy statement is crucial as it should explain the school's agreed intent in physical education and be based on National Curriculum requirements. It should summarise the school's philosophy (rationale) and aims and objectives, according to each Key Stage, and it is vital that this is agreed by staff, the headteacher and governors before any additional work takes place. The NEELB (1995) suggest:

> *A Physical Education Policy describes the purpose, nature and management of a PE programme in the school. It should cover the compulsory elements incorporated in legislation and describe the guiding principles which govern the place of Physical Education in the school curriculum. The PE Policy should set out the aims and objectives of the PE curriculum in your school. These should be in line and indeed complement the general*

aims of the school. A statement should recognise the place of PE within the Creative and Expressive area of study and the contribution it can make to this particular area. Perhaps an outline of the areas of commonality between the subjects within this area of study and also the unique contribution of PE.

Chapter 4 should help you clarify and confirm the aims of your PE curriculum and help you identify key phrases to explain you rationale.

When I read through a selection of school handbooks it was interesting to note that many were sound in detail but it was difficult to know when the documents were written, amended or revised. I think it is useful to place your curriculum statement in a context. Harrison (1995) suggests that coordinators should indicate how the policy has been prepared or at what state it is in at present:

 This policy is a result of a staff working party and discussion with the local adviser. It was agreed by all staff at a meeting held on . . . and subsequently agreed by governors on . . .

(p. 15)

You may find the following examples of existing school policies helpful.

FIG 7.3
Lime Kiln Primary School
curriculum statement

Aims of Physical Education
Physical education contributes to the overall education of young people by helping them to lead full and valuable lives through engaging in purposeful physical education. It can develop physical competence and help promote physical development. It can teach pupils, through experience, to know about and value the benefits of participation in physical activity while at school and throughout life. It can develop an appreciation of skilful and creative performance across the areas of activity.

Physical education can also contribute to the development of problem-solving skills. It can contribute to the establishment of self-esteem through the development of physical confidence. It can contribute to the development of interpersonal skills.

Physical activity is combined with the thinking involved in making decisions and selecting, refining, judging and adapting movements. Through these activities, pupils should be encouraged to develop the personal qualities of commitment, fairness and enthusiasm.

These broad aims have been drawn from the National Curriculum (1995) and form the basis for physical education planning at Lime Kiln.
It was revised September 1996.

FIG 7.4
Cranfield School PE policy

Physical Education Policy

Introduction
Physical Education is a foundation subject within the National Curriculum.
At Cranfield School it is our philosophy to give children an opportunity to:
- participate and develop their own levels of expertise;
- build relationships in meaningful situations with others; and
- increase their awareness of how their bodies work.

This policy outlines the purpose, nature and management of the Physical Education taught.

Rationale
Physical Education is concerned with the skilful management of the body. It aims to develop physical competence in order that children are able to move efficiently, effectively and safely in a variety of situations in such a way that they understand what they are doing. Learning through action is an essential skill developed alongside personal awareness and observation of themselves and others. The achievement of this by the children occurs through a combination of motor and cognitive development. The physical activity and mental processes of making decisions, judgments, selecting, refining, adjusting and adapting.
Involvement in the development process will enhance qualities such as commitment, fairness, tolerance and concern for others. It will also show each individual their own achievements and successes. Physical Education will make special and particular demands of the child which are not easily understood and developed in their curriculum subjects.

Aims
- To facilitate the development of children's body awareness.
- To enable children to apply and adapt a range of skills.
- To understand the concepts of the body and its response to exercise following practical experiences.
- To provide an introduction to a healthy and active lifestyle.
- To help children appreciate the joy of moving in practical and aesthetic ways.
- To develop individual personal and social skills to manage success and failure in competitive and cooperative situations.
- To extend each child's knowledge and understanding of sport and its heritage in our society.

At Cranfield school we believe that each child should have the opportunity for a balanced development through a range of opportunities and experiences. Our aims relate closely to the activity specific requirements of the National Curriculum and will be developed through the successful completion of the PE programme. The National Curriculum emphasises that all children must plan, perform and evaluate their work. The main emphasis at Cranfield will be on participation.

The following policy statements provide guidance for a whole school approach towards, for example, safety, equal opportunities, and extra-curricular provision.

FIG 7.5
Sample policy showing progressive use of apparatus

Apparatus Policy

1 Always progress slowly.

2 Work should be carried out on the floor before applying it to apparatus.

3 Progress slowly from the floor to small apparatus, to linked pieces of small apparatus, to medium pieces and finally to large apparatus.

4 Decide what apparatus is needed, and have it placed near to where it is to be used. This should be carried out before the lesson. (This could be carried out by class helpers during the introduction of the lesson.)

5 Plan the apparatus layouts in advance.

6 Allow enough time to develop the skills of sharing, lifting, carrying and placing small apparatus before progressing further.

7 Make sure every child knows how to lift, carry and place apparatus. Teachers should help with different pieces and should check all apparatus before use.

8 Ensure safety in the layout of apparatus. Make sure there is space around the apparatus and that it is arranged to encourage the children to start from a variety of places. Discourage queuing. Use appropriate height for children to work at. The use of coloured tape to denote specific heights could be used on climbing frames.

9 If necessary put apparatus away after each lesson.

10 Where apparatus is awkward to get out, it might be possible for the whole school to decide to work on gymnastics during a specific term. This would allow for all the equipment to be set out around the side of the hall for the duration of a day, week or even term, providing it was stored safely. This will save considerable time during gymnastics.

11 Avoid overcrowding — 4–6 children in each group.

12 Initially, each group sits in the same grid at the start of each lesson and brings out and puts away their own apparatus. When the children are ready, each group can bring out and put away different pieces of apparatus each week.

13 The children should sit on the floor away from the apparatus at the beginning and the end of each task. This prevents fidgeting with the apparatus and helps to focus attention on the task.

14 Set questions which will challenge the class to use both the floor and the apparatus.

15 Apply floorwork tasks to the apparatus in order to challenge the children's understanding of the movement tasks. Use words such as around, over, along, across, under, up, down and through. This will encourage variety and progression of the previously acquired movement techniques. Gradually build up your movement vocabulary on the apparatus.

(*Source:* NEELB, 1995)

FIG 7.6
Avondale School sample wet
weather policy

Wet Weather Policy
Perhaps the weather more than any other external factor is capable of disrupting the planned curriculum. This problem is heightened here due to the severe lack of indoor space at our disposal. What follows, therefore, is a policy that reflects our school circumstance.

When should outdoor lessons be abandoned?
1 When there is a potential risk to children's safety; if the surfaces are too slippery; or if the children do not have appropriate footwear for the activity.
2 If the teacher deems that the weather will have a detrimental effect on teaching and learning.
3 When the health of either party may be at risk.

Damage limitation to the curriculum
As far as possible, the activity done inside should reflect the timtabled activity either through a small game or skill session.
We prefer to keep lessons as performance orientated as possible. Therefore the activity provided as an alternative will be as physical as possible for the greatest number of children. We positively encourage the use of 'mass' fitness sessions — particularly where we have more than one class on at any one time.
We simply then endeavour to add on an extra session to the timetabled outdoor block so that the children do not miss out. Should the inclement weather persist, then it may be pertinent to bring forward an 'indoor' block and revert to the outdoor block at a later date.

| Chapter 8 | Developing a scheme of work |

The next section of your documentation is a scheme of work. This should detail the experiences that you intend, as a school, to provide for children across the Key Stages in order to achieve the aims and objectives of the school policy. The scheme should include aims and objectives underpinning the teaching and learning experiences as identified in Part Two.

Schemes of work

A scheme of work outlines the long-term planning for a particular period of time, usually a Key Stage, and should include themes or topics to be handled at various stages. It should be drawn up using the National Curriculum Statutory Orders, Programmes of Study and End of Key Stage Descriptors and will provide an overview of the physical education curriculum. However, the NC itself does not constitute a scheme of work; it indicates the minimum requirements and provides a framework that has to be interpreted and developed into a systematic scheme of learning experiences for children. Implementation, therefore, has to take account of the relevant policies and circumstances of every school.

The scheme should provide an overview of the wide range of activities that have been selected to
■ offer children a broad and balanced experience
■ provide progression and continuity
■ serve as a reference for all teachers

and this will 'align' and cross-refer to the aims listed in the National Curriculum PE Programme of Study statements. From this information, medium and short-term planning can be designed into units of work and lesson material.

The scheme of work must cover the Programmes of Study (PoS) for each Key Stage. In 1991 the National Curriculum working party defined the purpose of Programmes of Study: 'to establish the matters, skills and processes which children should be taught in order to achieve the Attainment Target' (DES, 1991, p. iii). Following significant revision, this now reads 'set out what pupils should be taught' (DFE, 1995, p. v). The scheme of work will also need to meet the statutory common and general requirements.

■ common requirements — the issue of access.
■ general requirements — to involve pupils in the process of performing, planning and evaluating with the emphasis on performance;
  to promote physical activity and healthy lifestyles;
  to develop positive attitudes;
  to ensure safe practice.

Constructing a scheme of work

Figures 8.1 and 8.2 are examples of two schemes of work. You will notice that a rationale is offered for each Key Stage along with an overview of the activities to be offered to pupils. At this stage the detail is very general. Firstly take your school aims and identify key objectives for each Key Stage. Next take the amount of time that you have available and fill in a Key Stage plan. Check this against the requirements:

1 At Key Stage 1, do you have three activity areas? Is the curriculum broad and balanced?
2 At Key Stage 2 do children experience all six areas?

The proformas included at the end of this chapter may be useful to conduct an audit of your scheme of work (see pp. 159–61).

Both of the Key Stage curriculum plans illustrate a very healthy amount of time and space allocated to PE. This may well be the 'ideal' and in your school there may be limited 'hall time' and this may well limit the number of PE lessons to two per week plus one in any other space. PE may also have to

FIG 8.1
Key Stage 1 PE curriculum plan

The early years are crucial in laying the foundations of physical competency and positive attitutes to physical activity. Pupils at this Key Stage should experience a variety of activities which develop a wide range of skills. A sense of fun, enjoyment and achievement should pervade all activities.

At the beginning of Key Stage 1, much activity will be exploratory play in which pupils, individually, with a partner, or in a small group, respond to suggestions of the teacher, or to the stimuli and challenges provided by music, space or apparatus. With guidance, the play will become more structured and lead to the development of skills.

Pupils should be allowed time to develop confidence, both as individuals and members of a group. They should learn to listen and respond to guidance from the teacher, and to talk about their experience in the physical education lesson.

Although presented in discrete activity areas, the programmes of study in the early years should be taught frequently as integrated lessons, using various movement themes in different contexts. As pupils develop skills in the areas of physical education, lessons should focus on developing skills in these specific areas.

YEAR	TERM	LESSON 1	LESSON 2	LESSON 3	LESSON 4
Year R (4/5 yr olds)	Autumn 1 Autumn 2	Games	Gymnastics	Dance	Dance
	Spring 1 Spring 2	Games	Gymnastics	Gymnastics	Dance
	Summer 1 Summer 2	Games	Gymnastics	Games	Dance
Year 1 (5/6 yr olds)	Autumn 1 Autumn 2	Games	Gymnastics	Games	Dance
	Spring 1 Spring 2	Games	Gymnastics	Dance	Dance
	Summer 1 Summer 2	Games	Gymnastics	Games	Dance
Year 2 (6/7 yr olds)	Autumn 1 Autumn 2	Games	Gymnastics	Games	Dance
	Spring 1 Spring 2	Games	Gymnastics	Gymnastics	Dance
	Summer 1 Summer 2	Games	Gymnastics	Games	Dance

FIG 8.2
Key Stage 2 PE curriculum plan

Building on the experiences gained during Key Stage 1, pupils should be given opportunities to develop their skills and apply them in more complex personal challenges. They should be given sufficient guidance to cope with these challenges. They should continue to experience success in order to reinforce a positive attitude to physical activity.

The exploratory approach should be continued but interspersed, more frequently, with guidance in order to achieve good quality performance in each of the areas of the programme of study. Pupils shoul be encouraged to discuss the physical activities and to develop an understanding of them and relationship to health and exercise in everyday life.

YEAR	TERM	LESSON 1	LESSON 2	LESSON 3
Year 3 (7/8 yr olds)	Autumn 1 Autumn 2	Outdoor Adventure Games Invasion	Gymnastics Dance	Gymnastics Dance
	Spring 1 Spring 2	Games Invasion Games Invasion	Gymnastics Dance	Gymnastics Dance
	Summer 1 Summer 2	Games Net/Racket Games Strike/Field	Dance Gymnastics	Games Net/Racket Games Strike/Field
Year 4 (8/9 yr olds)	Autumn 1 Autumn 2	Outdoor Adventure Games Invasion	Gymnastics Dance	Gymnastics Dance
	Spring 1 Spring 2	Games Invasion Games Invasion	Gymnastics Dance	Gymnastics Swimming
	Summer 1 Summer 2	Games Net/Racket Games Strike/Field	Athletics Athletics	Swimming Swimming
Year 5 (9/10 yr olds)	Autumn 1 Autumn 2	Games Net/Racket Games Invasion	Gymnastics Gymnastics	Swimming Dance
	Spring 1 Spring 2	Games Invasion Games Invasion	Dance Gymnastics	Swimming Swimming
	Summer 1 Summer 2	Games Net/Racket Games Strike/Field	Athletics Athletics	Dance Outdoor Adventure
Year 6 (10/11 yr olds)	Autumn 1 Autumn 2	Games Net/Racket Games Invasion	Gymnastics Dance	Gymnastics Dance
	Spring 1 Spring 2	Games Invasion Games Invasion	Gymnastics Dance	Gymnastics Dance
	Summer 1 Summer 2	Games Net/Racket Games Strike/Field	Athletics Athletics	Dance Outdoor Adventure

share space and time with other subjects. Many factors will affect the balance of your school curriculum and this must be shown in your scheme of work.

Units of work

The 'unit of work' is the medium-term part of the planning and represents a series of lessons, such as half a term or six weeks within a particular activity area. How material is organised will largely depend on the activity, theme or topic and whether it has to be planned as a specialist unit or with a cross-curricular focus. Objectives and learning outcomes need to be clearly defined. A clearly organised unit will make short-term planning of lessons much easier, in fact you may find it useful to plan individual lessons as part of the unit. This was reflected in the findings of Clark and Yinger (1987) whose research into teachers' planning concluded that unit planning appeared to be the most important aspect of planning for teachers.

Suggestion

Examine your school units of work. How much key information to they contain?
Do they offer a detailed step-by-step guide or a general over view?
How can you improve your unit of work?

When I looked at different examples of unit plans, it became evident that a unit of work needs to include the following key information:
Unit objective — which should also serve as the assessment criteria.
Content — details of the progressive content; main skills to be developed; the types of experiences to be offered; teaching methods approaches and learning activities.
Resources — equipment and materials required to effectively deliver the content.
Cross-curricular links — health and safety.
Assessment — learning outcomes; procedures.

Figures 8.3–8.6 are examples of medium-term plans, showing a variety of styles of presentation and different approaches to planning.

Whole school plan showing units of work for each area (Devon Curriculum Planning Advice).

Yr	DANCE			GYMNASTICS			GAMES			ATHLETICS			ADVENTURE ACTIVITIES			SWIMMING		
	AUT	SPR	SUM	AUT	SPR	SUM	AUT	SPR	SUM	AUT	SPR	SUM	AUT	SPR	SUM	AUT	SPR	SUM
R	Lets Move, Body Parts and Cross-Curric. Themes e.g. Alphabet Soup, Sweet Factory			Focus 1 + 2 TRAVELLING and STOPPING using hands and feet using large and small body parts (pp. 51-64)			Free choice — Restricted choice Sending, receiving and travelling with — Running and chasing games (pp. 29-54)											
1	Turning and Twisting, Dynamics and Cross-Curric. Themes e.g. Toy Factory; Nest Egg			Focus 2 + 3 TRAVELLING and STOPPING using large and small body parts/ ROCKING & ROLLING (pp. 58-71)			Specific skills input (pp. 55-63)	Simple games making e.g. Target Games (pp. 65-6)	Partners when ready (pp. 65-70)									
2	Relationships, Movement Patterns and Cross-Curric. Themes e.g. Bonfire Night, Jack and the Beanstalk			Focus 4 + 5 DIRECTIONS/ MOVING BODY PARTS at/to different levels (pp. 72-84)			Increased problem solving via games making target games, travelling with skills, net games, hitting, fielding and stopping (pp. 65-70)											
3	Dances from different times and places (including country dance)			Focus 6 + 7 FOCUS ON FEET AND LEGS — PATHWAYS AND LEVELS (pp. 89-103)			Net/ Racket + Invasion Games 1	Invasion Games Refer to (p. 28) Unit 2	Striking and Fielding (pp. 120-6)	ATHLETICS TO BE TAUGHT THROUGH GAMES			Going places Journeying		Planning and taking part — in 1 day Exped.	Water familiarisation — orientation (pp. 37-64)		
4	The Dance Pack — a topic-based approach e.g. The Fairground, The Sea			Focus 7 + 8 PATHWAYS AND LEVELS — BENDING, CURLING AND STRETCHING (pp. 97-110)			Net/ Racket + Invasion (pp. 87-101) Games 3	Invasion Games Unit 4 (p. 28)	Net/R (pp. 87-101) Striking Fielding (pp. 120-9)		Running, Jumping, Throwing through individual challenges (see p. 94)		Adopt a Path		Working together Outdoors	Stroke efficiency (pp. 64-71) Elements of survival technique		
5	The Dance Pack — a topic-based approach e.g. Dark and Light, Magnetism			Focus 8 + 9 BENDING, CURLING AND STRETCHING, — MAINTAINING SHAPE IN MOVEMENT (pp. 104-17)			Net/ Racket (pp. 87-109) Invasion Games 5	Invasion Games Unit 6 (p. 28)	Net/R (pp. 87-109) Striking Fielding (pp. 120-31)		Specific Running, Jumping, Throwing (p. 94)			Orienteering on school site — Initiative exercise		Stroke improvement (pp. 64-71) Survival and life saving skills (pp. 80-95) — Individual and activities (p. 71)		
6	The Dance Pack — a topic-based approach e.g. Maps and Pathways, Communication			Focus 10 + 11 CHANGING SPEEDS — SYMMETRY AND ASYMMETRY (pp. 118-31)			Net/ Racket (pp. 87-116) Invasion Games 7	Invasion Games Unit 8 (p. 28)	Net/R (pp. 87-116) Striking Fielding (pp. 120-34)		Specific Running, Jumping, Throwing, select from challenges (pp. 13-15)		Plan and undertake an overnight camp + Residential Experience (pp. 23-31)			Repetition and extension of for those pupils who have achieved the EofKS Statement		
7	Compose dances based on topics and ideas e.g. Greek Myths, Gang Warfare (p. 46). The Environment Sport			Focus 12 TRAVELLING WITH FOCUS ON PATHWAYS Focus 13 TWISTING TURNING AND SPINNING (pp. 136-43)			Net/ Racket + Invasion Games	Invasion Games (pp. 137-160)	Net/R (pp. 85-116) Striking Fielding (pp. 120-34)		Understand and apply techniques in a limited range of running jumping and throwing (personal and team		Developing techniques and specific skills in the Outdoors in one or more activities, either on or off site. Develop a variety of roles including leading, being led and sharing. (pp. 37-51)					
8	Learn set dances, including folk dances and compose own dances in the same style			Focus 14 MOVING INTO AND OUT OF BALANCE Focus 15 SWINGING AND CIRCLING (pp. 144-52)			Net/ Racket + Invasion Games	Invasion Games (pp. 137-160)	Net/R (pp. 85-116) Striking Fielding (pp. 120-34)		challenge in sustained and explosive events) (pp. 95-7)					2/4 recognised strokes on front back including starts, turns and finishes (pp. 64-71) Game forms and water based activities (pp. 71-80) Principles and practise of rescue and resuscitation (pp. 80-91) + pp. 141-9)		
9	Analyse and learn set dances using recognised dance forms e.g. ABA or Rondo, and compose own dances in the same style			Focus 16 LIFTING AND LOWERING Focus 17 FLIGHT (pp. 153-163)			Net/ Racket + Invasion Games	Invasion Games (pp. 137-160)	Net/R (pp. 85-116) Striking Fielding (pp. 120-34)		Some selection within bands of running jumping and throwing Use of group competition							

(Source: Devon Curriculum Planning Advice — page references relate to other documents)

FIG 8.3

Whole school plan showing units of work for each area

FIG 8.4
Key Stage 1: Medium-term Plan
— Unit of Work for Year 1 Dance

Unit 1: Ourselves: Select from the content below for 2–6 lessons.

Aims: To provide opportunities for pupils to:

- experience creating, performing and appreciating dance movements and dances working alone and in pairs through the following aspects of the programme of study;
- experience and develop control, coordination and elevation in basic body actions including travelling, jumping, gesture and stillness;
- body shape, size and space in the room;
- working with a range of stimuli including music;
- experience of dances with beginnings, middles and ends.

Lessons 1 and 2: Dances:

(i) My Feet (solo)
(ii) Our Feet (partner dance)

Main learning activities:

(a) parts of the feet isolated and in contact with the floor — flat, toes, heels, edges;
(b) jumping using feet in different ways;
(c) step patterns emphasising feet — hop, skip, leap, gallop, march, trudge, trot, prowl, etc;
(d) copying, leading and following partner.

Resources:
Music — a variety of short pieces (*BBC Radiophonic* or *Time to Dance* tape)

Lessons 3 and 4: Dance: Hands Dance (solo and partner)

Main learning activities:

(a) parts of hands touching each other and the floor;
(b) hands open, close, wide, narrow, pointed, spread, floppy, stiff (changing speed and tension);
(c) hands leading into travel, rise, fall, turn, dip, chase, etc;
(d) hands making clapping rhythms on own and with a partner contacting hands, floor and parts of the body.

Resources:
Pictures of South Asian dance hand gestures, video of Austrian Schuplattler Dance (if available), also music from these sources.

Lessons 5 and 6: Dance: 'Look What I Can Do!' (solo in group)

Main learning activities:

(a) Variety of travelling actions on feet and on different body parts e.g. rolling, sliding;
(b) Everyday actions (mime into dance) enlarging them e.g. dressing, working actions — digging, sweeping, cleaning, sawing, etc;
(c) Playing — e.g. ball, skipping rope;
(d) Rest — be still, sleep.

Resources:
Music e.g. Shostakovich gallops and polkas or any other lively pieces.

(*Source*: Smith-Autard, 1995, *Teaching PE at Key Stage One and Two*, pp. 39–40, PEAUK)

GAMES UNIT Reception	INTENTIONS: To give experience of using a variety of games equipment. To develop awareness of space and the safety factors based on the use of space. To introduce running and chasing games. To explore and introduce the skills of sending, receiving and travelling with a ball. TIME ALLOCATION: 40% of total PE curriculum time.	EKSD Pupils plan and perform simple skills safely. They improve their performance through practising their skills.

Learning Outcomes	Learning Activities		Focal Points
1. An awareness of the importance of using space with consideration for others. 2. Increased confidence in using a range of equipment. 3. Early development of sending, receiving and travelling with skills.	**Free Play/Free Choice** Child-centred exploration of equipment. Discovery of the range of action possibilities with a wide variety of equipment. Individual guidance and challenge to promote skill improvement. **Restricted Choice** Teacher-set challenges, guiding learning through a particular type of equipment or the development of a specific skill. Individual and group activities based on running and chasing to encourage children to develop core movement skills. Activities which encourage anticipation of movement of others.	**Key skills to work on:** *Sending* Rolling Throwing Kicking *Receiving* Self-feed — chasing and picking up Rebounding — from a wall or upturned bench Catching from a self-fed bounce or throw Trapping with feet *Travelling with* Dribble (with feet or hand) Run and carry Run, carry and avoid *Moving with awareness of others* Run, chase and avoid Run and stop Run and change direction Follow, copy	■ Can they find spaces into which to run? ■ Is there sufficient control to avoid collisions with other pupils or objects, and do so without falling over? ■ Does the child show age appropriate coordination in gross motor skills (running, throwing, jumping)? ■ Does the child show development in hand–eye coordination in receiving or hitting skills? ■ Is there a willingness to try out different pieces of equipment? ■ Does the pupil show imagination in equipment use? ■ Is there a willingness to practise a particular skill in order to improve? ■ Is there improvement in the handling and control of equipment, and in their movement in relationship to moving objects? ■ Are pupils able to watch others or demonstrate their own ideas and talk about them?

(*Source*: Spackman, Collin and Kibble, 1995, *Teaching PE at Key Stage One and Two*, pp. 8–12, PEAUK)

FIG 8.5
Medium-term plan for games unit for Reception class

Lesson planning

Planning lessons is the short-term stage of planning. Teachers will plan lessons in very different ways according to their experience and personal preference. In a study of experienced, effective primary teachers, Stroot and Morton (1989) discussed two general teacher types:

Plan dependent teachers — prefer to have access to lesson plans, to be able use them intermittently, take a 'glance' and this provided them with personal comfort and confidence.

Plan independent teachers — prefer to have a mental image of previous planning which has been internalised and provides them with a repertoire of information without needing to have it written down. (p. 212)

Allowing teachers to have freedom in the way they work at the delivery stage is important as they need to feel comfortable and at ease. As teachers generally become more experienced and confident their written planning becomes less detailed, but it remains as part of a mental map. When working with student-teachers and newly qualified teachers, I feel it would be more appropriate to have a policy which requires them to have detailed lesson planning which clearly outlines learning objectives, learning activities, class organization and management (including attention to teaching styles), concluding with evaluation. Mentors should therefore expect detailed plans.

What should be in a lesson plan?

Once again this will vary according to the learning objectives, related activities, teaching strategies, and organisation of time, pupils and resources. Figures 8.6–8.8 are examples of this level of planning.

The use of apparatus is a *big issue* in primary PE lessons, when to use it, how to use it, all of it, some of it, themed approach (i.e. apparatus suited to rotation, flight, etc.). One headteacher said he was constantly asked questions such as, 'How, when, why do we use the apparatus?' It is certainly a key issue for 'lay PE teachers' — the non-specialist in Key Stages 1 and 2. Detailed planning is the first stage in offering teachers some confidence in their teaching. An example can be found in Maude, 1995, p. 55.

	GROUP 1:	Confident, improvement of breast stroke — deep water.
GROUP 2:	Introduction to breast stroke — shallow water. Work on submerging.
NUMBER OF PUPILS:	10–15 pupils in each group. Helper available to work on the poolside.
EQUIPMENT:	Floats, sinkers, weighted hoops, tape recorder.
TEACHER'S AIM:	Improve confidence; development of the breaststroke technique.

	INTRODUCTION ACTIVITY	GUIDANCE	ORGANISATION
10 mins	Enter steps, jump from side — Group 1 deep end		Pool divided across by rope Music. Work to teacher's instructions. Helper guides individuals.
	1. Travel freely in space. When music stops a) tread water or float; b) rotate; c) bob up and down.	'Look for space' 'Keep feel off the pool floor' 'Encourage variety of movement'	
20 mins	**MAIN THEME**		
	1. All try to swim breast stroke — demonstration by selected pupil	'Glide to start' 'Head still' 'Blow hands away' 'Look at head position' 'Look at feet bent up and bend of knees' 'Legs even'	Pupils observe from pool side Ask pupils why
	Repeat breast stroke — apply points from demonstration	Individual guidance	Helper work with Group 1
	2. Breast stroke leg action Group 1 — Float ahead	'Narrow leg action' 'Heals to seat' 'Swirl and glide'	Helper — Group 1 organise into partners 1 width legaction ¹/₂ widths — out on back, return on front, 4 strokes each way
	Group 2 — Float ahead, work on even leg stroke and foot position head steady		
	3. Group 1 — Full stroke for 2 widths — at turn both hands on wall, good push off	'Concentrate on leg action' Individual help	Helper — Group 2 organise into Partner — 2 widths
	Group 2 — Full stroke	Individual help	Part 1 width
8 mins	**CONTRASTING ACTIVITY**		
	Group 1 — Push and glide under water	'Hips high, head between arms, good stretch'	
	— Weighted hoop: push through hoop, swim on	'Lift hands to surface' 'Blow out under water'	2 or 3 per hoop: hoop held down if no weighted hoop available
	Group 2 — Sinkers placed: recover with hands	Give time to experiment	
	Group 2 — observe successful attempts from poolside	'Why can they submerge?'	
	Progress to swim, collect object, swim on	Individual help 'Eyes open, hips high'	
2 mins	**CONCLUSION**		
	All — sculling, head leading and/or feet leading; stop in wide float	'Head back, hands by side' 'Strong tipping action'	Helper and teacher — Individual guidance

(*Source*: Elkington and Harrison, 1995, *Teaching PE at Key Stage One and Two*, pp. 67–8, PEAUK)

FIG 8.6
Swimming — Key Stages 1 and 2 — mixed ability — 2 groups

Intention: By the end of this lesson pupils should be able to throw with increased power and catch a high ball safely, and should be better at judging the flight of a ball they have thrown.

Pre-lesson organization: distribute enough small balls for one per pupil between three baskets.

Organization for Task 1: on arrival in the working area each pupil takes a ball from a basket.

Task (What pupils do)	Observations (What to look for)	Points to remember
Warm-up 'Hold your ball in one hand and jog in the area, changing directions as you go. Now bounce the ball on the ground and catch it as you travel. Now throw it above your head and catch it. Can you throw it up and catch it without having to stop or run faster to make the catch?'	Do pupils look up to avoid others? When throwing the ball up, how many can match their throw to coincide with their movement? Help them to throw the ball ahead and to move forward to catch it.	*Enabling idea*: have bean bags and slightly larger balls available.

Bridging organisation: divide the class into three fairly equal groups. Send group 1 to a wall, group 2 into a clear space and group 3 to an area with two lines with a 5–10 metre (16–33ft) gap between them. Provide a card at each station to set the task, or let the pupils play freely at their station while you visit each in turn to set the task.

Revision **Station at the wall**: Task 97 Catch the rebound (page 33). After a few practice turns at throwing, insist that the rebound is caught.	Do the pupils get sideways-on and take the hand well back as they prepare to throw? Does the elbow come away from the body as they throw? Does the hand follow through after the ball?	If pupils throw underarm, ask them to try overarm and to see which is the most powerful.
New work **Station in free space**: Task 88 Clap and catch (page 32).	Do pupils watch the ball throughout? Which throw goes highest — underarm or overarm?	Let pupils invent their own 'tricks' to perform while the ball is in the air.
New work **Station with two lines**: Task 91 Target catch (page 32). Throw the ball from behind one line across the gap and run to catch it on the far side of the second line.	Do they move smoothly into the fun from the throw? Can they judge the flight of the ball for height and length, and arrive in time to catch the dropping ball?	*Easier variation*: reduce the gap, and gradually extend it again with practice.
Rotate each group through each station with an equal period of time on each.		

Bridging organization: for the task that follows, only permit all the pupils to work freely at the same time if the space is large enough. Alternatively, require pupils to work in the same direction across an area so that all the throws are in parallel.

New work Player A with the ball says 'go' and counts out loud from one to five. On 'go' player B runs as far away as s/he can while staying within the boundaries of the area. When player A shouts 'five' player B has to stop and stand still. Player A throws the ball towards B and runs to catch it. How many throws does player A need to take before s/he can catch the ball, stand still and reach out to touch his/her partner with the ball? The ball must not touch the ground. Change over.	Do pupils wait for a space before throwing? Can they judge line and length? Help pupils to appreciate the relationship between power, trajectory, and the time the ball takes to cover a given distance.	If space is limited, be prepared to work the pupils in groups one after the other, in one direction, with recovery back round the outside of the area.

Closing organization: 'From where you are, see how few throws/catches you and your partner need to make before you can place your ball in a basket. If the ball touches the ground you go back and start again.'

Cool-down
'Gently jog on the spot with the toes only just leaving the ground; make each step lower until neither foot is leaving the ground, though each is being stretched as the weight goes up onto the toes and down again. Stand still and then walk slowly back to your classroom.'

(*Source*: Read and Edwards, 1992, *Teaching Children to Play Games*, p. 48, with permission of the English Sports Council)

FIG 8.7
Games lesson plan 2 — Familiarization and skill challenge

Year Reception Key Stage I	Lesson:	Intro	Middle	Late

Lesson Objectives:

To continue to work on using space safely.

To develop the receiving skill of catching.

Introductory Activity	**Focal Points**
1. Hoops, enough for one each, are scattered around the playground. Pupils run around the hoops until the teacher gives a signal, they must then step/jump into an empty hoop. Hoops can then be taken away, giving an incentive to find one quickly.	Is there a sufficient control to avoid collisions with other pupils, and do so without falling over?
2. This time the teacher calls out a number, and pupils have to get that number of people in each hoop.	Do pupils show development in hand–eye coordination in receiving skills?
Development	**Teaching Points**
1. With a beanbag each, pupils move around with it in different ways — on the head, shoulder, jumping with it between the feet etc.	■ Pupils should not be 'put out' of the first game as this would defeat the object of maximum activity to warm up. The teacher could ask who managed to get a hoop every time.
2. Holding it on hands held together and flat, they make it 'bounce' sending it a little higher each time and trying not to drop it.	■ Make use of the second activity for some practical number work.
3. Work on catching technique, throwing it in the air with one or two hands. Encourage throwing only as high as can be caught.	■ Catching tips:
4. Pupils try to do this whilst walking or running.	watch the beanbag/ball right into the hands;
	stand so that the sun is not shining in your eyes;
Concluding Activity	keep the two little fingers together;
What time is it Mr Wolf?	spread the fingers to give a bigger catching surface;
One person is 'Mr Wolf' and walks in front with his/her back to the others. They follow cautiously saying 'What time is it Mr Wolf?' He gives a time, but if he says 'dinner time', the group has to run back to the starting line. If caught by Mr Wolf, that pupil becomes the next Mr Wolf.	put fingers tightly around the beanbag/ball when it comes into the hands, 'to stop it getting away'.
	■ Use a beanbag filled with beans as opposed to foam pieces.
Extension Activities	**Facilitating Activities**
Encourage running whilst throwing and catching. Move on to a medium-sized ball, decreasing the size of the equipment as the skill develops.	Use a large beanbag to assist eye coordination.
	Discourage wild/high throwing which decreases the chances of successful catching.
	Encourage higher throwing for sound catching.

(*Source:* Spackman, Collin and Kettle, 1995, *Teaching PE at Key Stage One and Two*, p. 12, PEAUK)

FIG 8.8

Games lesson plan for reception class

Evaluating current provision

Good teaching practice involves reflection and appraisal (see p. 39). Any planning, be it a scheme of work, a unit or an individual lesson, should be evaluated in the light of experience, and can be specific or general. Don't be too ambitious and expect teachers to analyse every lesson plan in detail, select a realistic number. Encourage them to periodically review short-, medium- and long-term plans.

Look at your existing documents and evaluate the PE statement. Does it reflect your aims? Consult your school's scheme of work. Calculate the amount of time allocated to each activity area at each Key Stage and complete the following proforma. This will give you an overview of the time allocation for PE and will show at a glance what is being covered.

ACTIVITY AREA TOTAL % of time	KEY STAGE 1		KEY STAGE 2			
	YR. 1	YR. 2	YR. 3	YR. 4	YR. 5	YR. 6
ATHLETICS	25%	10%				
DANCE	25%	20%				
GAMES	25%	20%				
GYMNASTICS	25%	20%				
OUTDOOR AND ADVENTUROUS		10%				
SWIMMING		10%				

Is there balance of provision? Do you meet the requirements? What activites have the different Key Stages covered? In how much depth? You could develop an audit sheet, like the following example.

Avondale Middle School PE Audit

	Key Stage 1 Years 2, 3, 4			Key Stage 2 Years 5, 6		
	Covered in depth	Covered briefly	Not covered	Covered in depth	Covered briefly	Not covered
GAMES						
Baseball						
Basic ballskills						
Catching games						
Fielding/striking						
Hockey						
Pop lacrosse						
Mini basketball						
Mini cricket						
Netball						
Rounders						
Rugby						
Soccer						
Table Tennis						
Tennis						
Volleyball						
GYM						
Balance						
Flight						
Jumping						
Rotation						
Sequencing						
Using apparatus						
Weight on hands						
ATHLETICS						
Fartlek training						
High jump						
Long jump						
Measuring/recording						
Pace change						
Sprint start						
100m						
200m						
400m						
600m						
800m						
1500m						
Throwing						
– ball						
– discus						
– javelin						
– shot						
Standing long jump						
Standing high jump						

	Key Stage 1 Years 2, 3, 4			Key Stage 2 Years 5, 6		
	Covered in depth	Covered briefly	Not covered	Covered in depth	Covered briefly	Not covered
OAA						
Abseiling						
Canoeing						
Caving						
Climbing						
Orienteering						
Trust games						
SWIM						
Swimming Skills						
DANCE						
Creative						
Cultural						
Measuring/recording						
Set dance						
HRF KNOWLEDGE						
Aerobic fitness						
C/down						
Endurance						
Flexibility						
Healthy eating						
Strength						
W/up						

Part four Monitoring for Quality

Chapter 9
Monitoring and assessing
children's achievement

Chapter 9   Monitoring and assessing children's achievement

During the early 1990s there was a great deal of public and political discussion about two issues: the standards of performance of our national teams; and the fitness levels of young people. As a result PE came under the microscope, with attention directed at an alleged decline in standards of achievement and attainment in our schools. Accountability also emerged as a buzzword, with parents, governors, politicians, HMI inspectors and the general public all wanting to know about standards, and if the curriculum was being adequately delivered. While I do not want to enter into a debate about the rights and wrongs of accountability here, we do need to acknowledge that current working conditions include statutory assessment that is scheduled to be externally 'audited'. The potentially most far-reaching influence on pupils' achievement and assessment was the implementation of the National Curriculum in Physical Education (DES, 1992, DFE, 1995). This formalised expectations at the end of four key stages along with programmes of study and a specified attainment target, all of which have since become a way of life in schools.

Types of assessment

Diagnostic: to scrutinise areas of learning in order to provide the appropriate feedback, support and guidance.

Formative: to ensure that ongoing achievements are recognised, directional feedback is given, and the next stages in learning are planned.

> **Summative:** to record the overall achievement and progress of a child in a systematic and meaningful way at the end of a particular phase. It will accurately inform other teachers, parents, and most importantly, the child concerned.
>
> **Evaluative:** to provide a systematic procedure for curriculum review and to acknowledge, achievements and development targets.

As PE coordinator you will be central to the design and implementation of any policy related to the assessment and monitoring of children's achievement or attainment in your school. This may be neatly summarised in the coordinators' job description as

> *Assess children's progress, maintain and provide written reports to parents in accordance with LEA and school policies.*

This is further inforced by the TTA (1996) proposals for the role of subject leaders, who they suggest should

> *Establish short, medium and long term plans for the development and resourcing of the subject, which ensure coverage, continuity and progression for all pupils including those with special educational or linguistic needs. Establish and implement clear policies and practices for assessing, recording and reporting on pupil achievement and the implementations of these policies and practices for the future teaching of the subject.*
>
> *Monitor and evaluate progress and achievement in the subject by all pupils, including those with special educational needs, taking action as necessary to raise achievement and setting clear targets for improvement, taking account of relevant local and national information.* (p. 7)

With this in mind this section is designed to provide you with relevant knowledge about current debate and practice in PE, the expectations for pupils' achievement in PE and how this can be assessed, recorded and reported. It addresses the why, what, when and how of assessment. First, I focus on the differences in practice and address the question, 'Why assess in PE?'

There is plenty of evidence both from OFSTED findings
and my discussions with practitioners which suggests that
many teachers, regardless of what age group they teach, find
assessment in PE difficult. Consequently, some design complex
assessment systems whilst others try to avoid doing it in any
systematic way. In one of my case study schools I found little
assessment going on in PE. When I asked the coordinator, 'Can
you tell me what you do for assessment', she replied:

 *Well, to be honest it's not done. In the scheme of work I have
put ideas, simple things to do. Tick sheets. The only real assessment is reports at the end of term. All the coordinators offer a
framework and set up a bank of statements that teachers use. I
don't think any other assessment is done. It's down to time. In
Years 5 and 6 maths and English are seen as the most important.*

This may be typical. However, in another school, a teacher's
response to the same question indicated that not only were
they looking at the physical aspect but had begun to focus on
other areas as well.

 *Assessment, oh we use a tick-off chart usually looking at skills.
Can they throw a ball? yes/no. Can they catch a ball? yes/no.
That sort of thing. They also do evaluations a couple of times
a term. The children have a review book and one week it might
be looking at PE so we get quite a lot of evaluation and it tells
us what the children think as well as how they are developing
their evaluating skills.*

My interview with the local primary OFSTED inspector
also revealed assessment as 'one difficult area'. In 1993,
the OFSTED report on inspectors' findings concluded:

 *In Key Stages 1 and 2 there was some evidence of sound
assessment, recording and reporting procedures in a few
schools, but in the majority one or more of these procedures
were inadequate. Many teachers lacked the confidence and
expertise to establish clear criteria for the assessment of pupils'
movement.* (DES, 1993, p. 13, para. 24)

For some teachers, PE will inevitably pose problems,
particularly as the subject-specific guidance has been very slow

coming from SCAA. They may gain some comfort from the knowledge that even PE specialist primary and secondary colleagues experience problems:

> ❝ *Good practice in recording of attainment and progress was hard to find and relatively few teachers had a clear vision of what system might be most appropriate . . . The survey revealed that only a few systems effectively linked teaching and learning objectives to the assessment criteria used.*   (OFSTED, 1995, p. 14)

Many teachers see the emphasis on assessment as an intrusion into their teaching. During my interview with colleagues, several main issues about assessment in PE emerged:

- lack of subject knowledge
- so much happens so quickly
- an erosion of activity time (with PE scheduled only twice a week often disrupted by bad-weather, double-booked facilities etc.)
- large numbers of pupils in any one class
- why bother? PE is supposed to be fun.

This tells us a lot about PE, as assessment is an integral part of primary school activities. Teachers already have a good deal of knowledge about how to monitor achievement and carry out assessment, which they constantly draw upon in their classroom practice. It is important for you to draw upon these existing skills and endeavour to encourage teachers to apply them to the, often alien, field of PE. You will need to help teachers to create time for assessment through the use of different teaching styles and learning opportunities.

It is for the PE coordinator in consultation with the headteacher to decide on how best to manage assessment in terms of:
- *what* — how many areas of activity?
- *when* — how often?
- *how* — consistency across Years and activities

The first stage is to audit current practice.

Suggestion

Look at the assessment systems you have in place, the policy and any record sheets. How well does your system work? Do you have any personal concerns? Do your colleagues have any concerns? Is your assessment linked with your schemes of work?

When reviewing your assessment process ask yourself and colleagues the basic question, 'Why do we assess in PE?' A short and simple answer 'Because we have to, it is statutory' is inadequate. While some colleagues may be cynical about this, I doubt whether any one would disagree with the idea that we need to determine children's progress, achievement, strengths, weaknesses and needs. Lou Veal (1992) talked about 'real' PE that focuses on pupils' learning, noting that whenever pupils participate in an activity under the supervision of a teacher there is always some form of assessment taking place. The assessment may be of behaviour generally (personal, social and moral); of on-task activity (response, application, and concentration); assessment of learning; of attainment and achievement (planning, performing and evaluating). Assessment is ongoing: as pupils work so the teacher observes and assesses performance (diagnostic assessment), usually offering feedback. Assessment is both formal and informal, structured and unstructured, planned and unplanned and is used to carefully shape the next part of the lesson and identify targets for individuals and classes (formative assessment). Assessment is also continuous, it is not something that is added at the end of a unit of work or end of a key stage — as Carroll (1994) comments, 'It is the very essence of what schools are in business for' (p. 4).

There are a number of reasons why we must recognise that assessment is integral to all teaching and learning. It is

 ... at the very heart of the process of promoting children's learning providing feedback and feed-forward.

(Raymond and Rolfe, 1994, p. 6)

It all relates to the questions, 'How do I know that the children are learning what I want them to learn as a result of my teaching?' 'How do I know what the children are achieving in PE?' Whatever the reasons underpinning assessment, it is useful to remember that 'assessment is essentially provisional, partial, tentative, exploratory and, invariably incomplete' (Drummond, 1993, p. 14) — it is not an end in itself, but a means to an end.

All of this relates to why we should assess and provides us with a set of general principles to guide practice. These are summarised below and remind us of the close interaction between the teacher, pupil and the subject in the process of teaching and learning. Ultimately it is the responsibility of the class teacher to create an appropriate teaching and learning environment, with assessment as an integral part. It is the class teacher who has to determine the what and how to assess and how the methods selected can be built into normal practice. It is your job as coordinator to help them achieve this.

ASSESSMENT PRINCIPLES
- Assessment should form a natural part of teaching and learning activities.
- Assessment activity should arise from current classroom practice.
- Assessment should build upon a child's previous experience.
- Assessment should relate to the learning outcomes identified in the objectives or specific tasks set within the classroom.
- Assessment should match the child's abilities.
- Assessment should be a shared process with the child, she/he needs to know *what* is expected and *why* their learning environment has been structured in specific ways.
- Assessment should *involve* the child who should be challenged to reflect critically on her/his learning in terms of the *process* involved and the *product* achieved.
- Assessment should focus on whether the learning outcome(s) match the curricular intention(s)

Designing and planning a policy for assessment

Subject coordinators have an important role to ensure that colleagues are not only aware of the school's subject policy on assessment of pupils' achievement, but how it works and whether it is effective. The policy must be easy to use and manageable for everyone.

Furthermore, assessment must inform teaching and curriculum planning — an area which OFSTED (1995) are keen to improve through inspection. A well thought-out and planned assessment policy will:
- provide us with valuable information about our children;
- in an era of accountability, it will allow us to share objective information about what our children are learning;
- help us evaluate the effectiveness of our programme;
- promote a whole school approach.

Schools should promote the quality of teacher assessment through a range of strategies, whilst avoiding unnecessary workloads for teachers (SCAA, 1996, p. 6).

It will require you to be a role model:

> ❝ *Lead by example through demonstrating and achieving high standards in their teaching of the subject which sustain and raise standards of pupil achievement, behaviour and motivation.*
>
> (TTA, 1996, p. 7)

This will require professional knowledge and understanding of:

> ❝ *National standards of achievement in their field and the position of their own school and pupils in relation to these standards.*
>
> (TTA, 1996, p. 10)

To help you untangle this complex area, the next section will do two things. Firstly it will examine pupils' achievement in PE. This links with the *aims* of PE programmes as identified in Chapter 2, while recognising the requirements of the NC and OFSTED. This clearly illustrates the need for planning and structuring learning and assessment together. Secondly, it will focus on the *process* of assessment: what is recognised as good practice, the importance of recording and reporting; and the linking of assessment to teaching and curriculum planning.

When considering all of this it is worth taking advice from the Hereford and Worcester County Council Physical Education Guidelines (1992, p. 51) which remind coordinators of three things:
- not everything you teach needs to be assessed;
- not everything you assess needs to be recorded;
- not everything you record needs to be reported.

What do we need to assess?

The Statutory Order for Physical Education (PE) is less prescriptive than many other subjects, so it is open to creative interpretation. Whilst this can be an advantage, it does mean that all teachers in all schools have to know what the requirements mean for their school curriculum and assessment practice. Your role in this is central for you will need to coordinate this interpretation and be able to illustrate how the requirements are being met. You will need to

> ❛ *Set expectations for staff and pupils in relation to standards of pupils achievement and the quality of teaching, establishing clear targets for improving and sustaining pupil achievement.*
>
> (TTA, 1996, p. 8)

It is also worth reminding ourselves that PE is different to other subjects because there are no SATs and no levels, just a single attainment target. While you might expect a single attainment target — which describes the 'type and range of performance that the majority of pupils should characteristically demonstrate by the end of the key stage . . .' (DES, 1995, p. 11) — to be straightforward, the attainment target actually summarises up to six programmes of study that define the knowledge, skills and understanding which all pupils are expected to have at the end of each Key Stage.

The PE policy will shape the school's scheme of work for PE which will clearly detail the different activities pupils are expected to learn. This provides the *criteria for assessment*. As a school, you may wish to assess children's capacities beyond the NC and include other related work, but whatever is decided you will need to provide all class teachers with guidelines on what pupils are expected to achieve. Much of this will also need to be available for reference during any OFSTED school inspection.

National Curriculum End of Key Stage Descriptors (EKSD) outlined on pp. 173–4 are summative, they require purely age-related judgments which should not take consideration of perceived potential or ability. Pupil attainment is compared with the national expectation across a specific age range, known as *norm referencing*, and assists the government in rank ordering a school's standard of achievement. Teachers must also consider the pupils' relative strengths and weaknesses across different aspects of the subject and also significant variations in attainment amongst different groups of pupils e.g. SEN, ethnic minority groups, different genders. The aim of End of Key Stage teacher assessment is for a rounded judgment which:

> *is based on knowledge of how the child performs across a range of contexts;*
>
> *takes into account strengths and weaknesses of the child's performance;*
>
> *is ... the closest match to the child's performance in each attainment target.* (SCAA, 1996a, p. 6)

In Part Two I outlined the potential aims of PE and detailed the knowledge, skills and concepts of each activity area. PE is now recognised as more than technical competence, more than the imitation and reproduction of skill. Children are to be provided with opportunities that allow them to develop techniques, and strategies, to solve problems, to create and compose movement, and to evaluate their own and others' performance — all of which are intended to assist their knowledge and understanding. To achieve this, teachers will need to look carefully at the learning environment that they are providing for their pupils. They will need to assess pupils' achievement in:

- performing;
- planning;
- evaluating.

For the under-5s, OFSTED will evaluate six areas of learning:

- language and literacy;
- mathematics;
- knowledge and understanding of the world;
- physical development;
- creative development;
- personal and social development. (OFSTED, 1996, p. 4)

Teachers should use the assessment evidence collated during a Key Stage to make a summative judgment about their pupils' achievement in relation to the EKSDs outlined below:

Key Stage 1 (Years 1–2)
Pupils plan and perform simple skills safely, and show control in linking actions together. They improve their performance through practising their skills, working alone and with a partner. They talk about what they and others have done, and are able to make simple judgment. They recognise and describe the changes that happen to their bodies during exercise.

It must be remembered that formal statutory requirements are likely to change and it is important that the coordinator considers this and keeps up to date with current documents.

Key Stage 2 (Years 3–6)
Pupils find solutions, sometimes responding imaginatively, to the various challenges that they encounter in the different areas of activity. They practise, improve and refine performance, and repeat series of movements they have performed previously, with increasing control and accuracy. They work safely alone, in pairs and in groups, and as members of a team. They make simple judgments about their own and others' performance, and use this information effectively to improve the accuracy, quality and variety of their own performance. They sustain energetic activity over appropriate periods of time, and demonstrate that they know what is happening to their bodies during exercise.

Additionally, consideration needs to be given to the inclusion of the statutory 'general' requirements; these outline what children should experience in relation to developing safe practice, positive attitudes, and independent learning. This would also ensure that during an OFSTED inspection documents would be readily available and an observer would instantly see the relationship between content and National Curriculum assessment requirements.

Spackman (1995) emphasises the need for teachers to *internalise* the expectations associated with an EKSD and the categories of attainment against which pupils will be judged. If you know that this is not currently the case for your colleagues then you should endeavour to structure a meeting or conduct a training session which allows them to get together and share their ideas and observations of children's attainment. You can then work together to agree a set of standards or expectations that will help to establish consistency and accuracy across the Key Stages.

Developing appropriate criteria which relate to the objectives of the unit of work which in turn relate to EKSD (see Part Three, pp. 153–4, for example documents) will help to inform teachers' assessment. Informed about the criteria for quality, teachers can go on to devise qualitative categories of criterion statements. These should be:
- clear statements, which are qualitatively different;
- concise but substantial;
- useful in a range of settings;
- true to the nature of the activity.

Suggestion

Look at your existing documents. Are the learning objectives clearly stated? Do teachers assess how well the children meet the objectives?

Teachers must use informed judgment and interpretative reasoning to apply the criteria to the assessment of children's work. The chart below offers some guidance on looking for evidence of quality in performance, planning and evaluation.

The following are evidence of quality performance:
accuracy — e.g. of application of body tension; appropriateness of response
efficiency — e.g. coordinated movement
consistency — e.g. sustained quality in repeated performance
adaptability — e.g. performing the learned skill in different contexts
ability to do more than one thing at a time
good design or pattern
effective expression
sustaining participation

The following are evidence of quality planning and organisation:
clear action leading to successful outcome
appropriate solution to task
safe performance
imaginative performance

The following are evidence of ability to evaluate performance:
selecting key features
making appropriate comparisons with other and/or previous performances
expressing pleasure in performance
sound judgments based on accurate observation

(Hereford and Worcester, 1992, p. 61)

How do we collect and record evidence?

Assessment should provide evidence of attainment, or lack of attainment. Evidence of attainment should provide 'proof' that a pupil has successfully achieved, on repeated occasions, an identified learning objective. Recognising and identifying achievement in PE is challenging because much of what happens in PE is transitory — few repeated performances are ever exactly the same.

As a teacher's evidence base is collected throughout the term, a considerable amount of information can accumulate. Whilst this will help develop a real understanding of what pupils can do, you should encourage them to record only key examples of attainment on a master sheet. This is particularly so when so many teachers have classes of up to 30 pupils and more.

Encourage your colleagues to occasionally record interim grades against each pupil's name. By doing this they will be able to identify pupils that may need more help and these can be observed over future weeks. Remind them of the pitfalls of developing a stereotype of a particular pupil and to guard against categorising pupils as being satisfactory because they try hard, *this is not achievement and it is important to recognise this difference.*

What and how teachers assess will depend on their knowledge of the various purposes and types of assessment relating to the children's work. The teacher should use methods that will not disrupt the lesson as the importance of the natural interrelationship between teaching, learning and collecting evidence for assessment cannot be overemphasised. The methods used should really be no different to those already employed in other subject areas, with which they will already be familiar. For example:

- **Talking** to children individually or in groups as they are working or reflecting on their work.
- **Listening** carefully to what children say as they discuss the tasks set or as they evaluate their own work or the work of others.
- **Observing** children throughout the process and during the performance of their work.
- **Looking** at a video of the children planning/composing and performing their work.
- **Analysing** written work in children's personal diaries, the class log book, or written notes, diagrams and records of their work.
- **Reflecting** on relevant information contained in the children's profiles and records.

As PE is essentially about practical performance, assessment must necessarily rest mainly upon observational skills, which most teachers already possess. Teachers are constantly collecting evidence of pupils' attainment through direct observation of pupils working: looking at how well they

Remember: Teachers are not required to assess everything and it is not necessary to even attempt to do so.

respond to tasks; their level of performance; their ability to explore and use materials, resources, equipment; how they are able to listen and talk to others; questioning pupils directly about their work. But these intuitive observations of the teacher will need to be focused if they are to provide a system capable of collecting and reproducing appropriate assessment information. It is also essential that the key role of observation is supported by a framework of other assessment methods which enable the teacher to compile evidence to justify the conclusions of their observations.

You should check, from time to time, that the evidence collected by the teacher relates to whether pupils have met the assessment criteria. For example, in games, does the evidence show that the pupils can demonstrate elements of games play that include running, chasing dodging and avoiding (Key Stage 1 games) or link a series of actions (Key Stage 1 gymnastics) or compose and control their movements by varying shape, direction, levels, speed and continuity. It is important for teachers to realise that the assessment process is integral to teaching and planning, and that it should be as simple as possible. This is endorsed by OFSTED (1995):

> *In general too many of the schools were attempting to do too much.* (p. 13)

During my interviews with coordinators it became evident that a key concern is that any system must be effective, make good use of time, with the emphasis on simple recording systems which teachers find easy to use. They expressed a need for strategies that are:

- easy to understand;
- clearly related to the scheme of work;
- easy to administer;
- simple in format.

Pupils need to be involved in assessment and should know at the outset what they are working towards; the learning outcomes; the assessment methods; and they need to know what it is they are expected to know, understand and do! Involving pupils in their own assessment is a requirement at all Key Stages. The Schools Examination Assessment Council (SEAC) (1991) suggest that

> ❛ Pupils can be actively involved in their own assessment: reviewing their work and progress; setting future targets for learning; and deciding in discussion with teachers, which pieces of work provide evidence of particular attainment. (p. 15)

If we are looking to make children independent then this must surely be part of our ongoing practice. Pupils will have to be taught how to assess and the purposes of self-assessment made clear to them. They must understand the language and criteria used and feel that the process is not just a personal process but will be commented upon by the teacher. This may involve some teachers adopting new teaching and learning styles, including reciprocal teaching — setting a range of open-ended and closed tasks — which involve pupils in evaluation and assessment. At the same time different styles of teaching will provide opportunities for the teacher to stand back and collect evidence. You may wish to use this as a topic for an INSET day.

How is evidence to be recorded and reported?

Collecting and recording evidence is one of the biggest concerns amongst teachers, primarily due to the administrative requirements. The exact means of recording evidence will depend on the policies that individual schools have in place. The Non Statutory Guidance (NCC, 1992) states that 'how' to record is a professional matter that should not be allowed to become too time consuming or to interfere with teaching activities. It is therefore for each school to adopt those methods they find most suitable to record evidence of a pupil's level of achievement. Methods of recording might include:

- video of work in progress/or the final product;
- photographs;
- checklists;
- children's Record of Achievement (ROA).

It should be noted that:

- the recording system must be easy to use and efficient;
- evidence recorded must relate to the tasks set and the end of key stage statement against which teachers are to report;
- children's achievements need to be systematically and regularly recorded.

It is important here to reiterate that teachers will not be able to record all the evidence all of the time. Teachers are generally concerned about the lack of time for assessment because they already have full timetables, little or no non-contact time, and constant personal demands made on them. Making time for assessment is important, but keep the system 'easy' and encourage colleagues to build it into their lessons. This means that they will be gathering evidence all the time, and will need to develop teaching styles which encourage children to work independently, thus creating time for the teacher to stand back, make interim judgments and record evidence which may be used towards the end of Year or Key Stage report.

Spackman (1995, p. 33) offers a sample recording sheet which can be used to note pupil progress and attainment, this is illustrated with some information for example

> **PE RECORD OF PROGRESS AND ATTAINMENT**
> NAME: A Arundel   KEY STAGE: 1
> UNIT DETAILS   EVIDENCE
> Gymnastics   basic actions achieved
>   some basic linking of skills

It may be worth considering the Schools Integrated Management System (SIMS) database package. This type of system is initially time consuming to set-up, but once in place it is quick and easy to use. The system records, in abbreviated form, individual pupil information which can then be printed out to provide a narrative for the pupil Record of Achievement. Helping teachers to find a system of recording that is suitable for all situations — the dance studio, gymnasium, sports hall and playing fields — is perhaps the most difficult task.
An exemplar is offered on page 180.

Reporting

The final stage of reporting is how the information is presented to pupils and parents. It is recommended that reporting should be essentially descriptive and, according to Non Statutory Guidance (NCC, 1992), comments should relate to the End of

Avondale Middle School Physical Education Department KS2 Assessment Record Pupil Profile						− − weak √ − average + − above average O − outstanding							A − Asthma T − Team D − Diabetic C − Club E − Epileptic I − Interform H − Heart O − Other ↓ ↓	
Class Name	invasion games	net/wall games	striking/ fielding games	dance	gymnastics	athletics track	athletics field	problem solving activities	general effort level	knowledge of H.R.F.	cooperation skills	safety	health problems (see key)	team representation extra curricular participation

FIG 9.1
An example of a record of achievement

Key Stage Statements, now known as Descriptors, and what the pupil has achieved in the Programme of Study. The Records of Attainment will then need to be translated into a pupil- and parent-friendly document which makes sense and is easily understood.

Most schools already use a standard pupil Record of Achievement for reporting achievements at the end of each Year, and the procedure and record adopted for PE should be the same. You could adapt Figure 9.1 for your own use.

What do our assessments tell us?

I recently looked at a colleague's grades for his children in PE and noticed that everyone had been awarded 'C' grade. With a class of 24 I thought this was virtually impossible and I was concerned that the methods of assessment had not drawn out the differences in levels of performance which were sure to

Suggestion

How often do you look at your pupils' grades and discuss them? If you scrutinise your Year 3 classes and see that everyone is achieving grade B or above, what does this mean for the next unit?

Are there any signs that some children may be underachieving?

Are there any patterns suggesting that one group may be disadvantaged? e.g. girls

Are you challenging and extending your pupils levels of achievement?

exist in such a large group. Discussion with my colleague was very open and honest and he admitted that he 'hadn't noticed' and had not really thought about it, 'but now that you mention it . . .' Further examination of the grades led to greater differentiation in future work and students identified as 'coasting' were challenged to achieve.

Integrating assessment into the teaching and learning process is evidently a complex and challenging task. Developing this practice will depend on the level at which you and your colleagues are working. The NC only offers a framework, to be interpreted by you and your colleagues to meet you own school requirements. A carefully planned curriculum, once designed, provides all the evidence of attainment needed.

Drummond (1993) encapsulates the role of effective assessment as

 . . . a process in which our understanding of children's learning, acquired through observation and reflection, can be used to evaluate and enrich the curriculum we offer. (p. 13)

It is never complete but is ongoing, integral to all our work.

STEPS TO MAKING AN ASSESSMENT POLICY

	What are you assessing? programmes of study/units of work
WHAT do you want pupils to learn?	What is the assessment for? What do children actually do? Do we provide the right learning opportunities?
HOW do you know they have learned it?	What are the assessment criteria? What judgments can we make?
HOW do you collect evidence?	What information do we need to collect? How? observation, videos, etc

HOW do you record pupils' learning?	Master record sheets for pupils and teachers.
HOW do you report to parents and to pupils?	Annual reports, pupils' profiles and records of achievement.

MONITORING AND EVALUATION OF ASSESSMENT
What do we do with the outcomes?
What happens after assessment?

Part five Resources for teaching and learning

Chapter 10   Managing resources: equipment and facilities

In its broadest sense 'Managing Resources' could include people, time, money and materials; this chapter concentrates on the last two as the others have been dealt with earlier in this book.

Physical education by its very nature needs a variety of specialist facilities, equipment and teaching materials. These may be on or off-site, indoor or outdoors, and vary in cost and maintenance needs. The OFSTED (1995) summary of good practice, reported on equipment and accommodation and clearly acknowledges very positive provision of resources:

> *Primary schools were generally well equipped for Physical Education work . . . the choice of good quality equipment had paid dividends. Most had chosen apparatus carefully, to take account of the wide-ranging needs of 5 year olds and 11 year olds of varying ability in the same school. The range of equipment was seen to be as important as its quantity, and these enthusiastic schools had been prepared to invest quite heavily in Physical Education.* (p. 18)

> *The picture was less positive in the area of accommodation where deteriorating areas presented the greatest potential difficulty.* (p. 9)

However the OFSTED inspections findings of 105 primary schools in 1993 declared

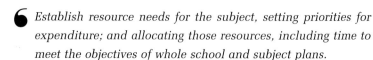

> *There was usually sufficient basic equipment for pupils . . . In some schools more appropriate apparatus was needed for Key Stage 1 pupils. When resources are less than satisfactory it was due to a shortage of finance, and on other occasions due to a lack of vision of what was required. Some primary schools still had very heavy gymnastic equipment which Key Stage 1 pupils, in particular, could not manage themselves.*
>
> (DES, 1993, p. 19)

This report clearly raises a number of issues for the coordinator, who is responsible for managing these resources and ensuring that they are as sufficient and appropriate as finance and vision allows. The TTA (1996), in their proposals for the role of subject leaders, define this responsibility as:

> *Establish resource needs for the subject, setting priorities for expenditure; and allocating those resources, including time to meet the objectives of whole school and subject plans.*
>
> *Create an effective and safe working and learning environment.*
>
> *Ensure the effective and efficient management and organisation of accommodation and learning resources including information technology.*
>
> *Maintain existing resources and explore opportunities to develop new resources from a wide range of sources inside and outside the school.*
>
> (p. 9)

This will involve a number of practical tasks such as stocktaking, monitoring, replacement and maintenance and most of all making sure things are available to the right people at the right time. This chapter looks at what managing equipment and facilities involves and offers some ideas on how you can fulfil your duties effectively and efficiently.

What is the coordinator's responsibility?

Start by checking with the headteacher the extent of your involvement in managing the resources for physical education. You may find that s/he assumes responsibility for the

Suggestion

How do you currently manage the PE resources?

What do you do now and how successful is it? Can you put your hands on an inventory of PE resources etc.? How up-to-date is it? Does it have a date? Do you do everything yourself and just get on with the job, or do you involve colleagues?

maintenance of large facilities and that your role revolves around equipment, apparatus and curriculum materials. Once this is established you can get to grips with doing your job. Most coordinator job descriptions are rather vague and general in detail, but demanding in practice. Headteachers will usually have expectations of you to keep an overview of resources and manage the budget.

Most primary colleagues will be happy to let you get on with the job, and will only get involved when they want something which is not there. However, long-term development in PE should really involve as many colleagues as possible in decision making about resources, even if it is at an information level, as it may help them appreciate the complexity and needs of the subject.

Consistency in management will also evolve from policy and procedures agreed by all or the majority of staff. (Details of policy design and examples of school policies are discussed in Part Three.) If you are to develop a whole school approach it is important to have agreed policies which also identify the way the school has agreed to manage its resources. These policies will shape the way you set about managing the resources and the budget allocated to PE.

Consider the two policies below and consider the strengths and weaknesses of each. They reflect different depths of content — How much do you think teachers, pupils, parent, governors and OFSTED need to know? What should feature in the policy and what should feature in details of organisation and management? There are also issues regarding the safety of stored equipment (shed on the field) and the emphasis on one game (football — boys and girls?) so obvious in the statements.

> **PRIMARY SCHOOL 1**
> **POLICY STATEMENT ON EQUIPMENT**
> In general, gymnastic equipment is kept in the store located in the school hall, games equipment is stored in the wooden shed on the games field, and small equipment such as skipping ropes, bats, small balls, etc. are kept in the sports hall store.
> Please play your part in keeping these stores tidy!

PRIMARY SCHOOL 2
RESOURCES POLICY STATEMENT

Cranfield school has excellent facilities for PE — large hall, playground with court and other games marking, a large field marked out for football and athletics in respective terms with a long/high jump pit too. There is a good selection of apparatus to use in the hall for gymnastics work and this is stored along the side of the hall and is easily manoeuvred by staff and children. The smaller equipment for use in other activity areas by both Key Stages is stored in boxes and racks on the shelves near the entrance to the hall. Here there is a large selection of small apparatus which can be used by both Key Stages. A good range of colour-coded equipment in many sizes is available. There are certain pieces of equipment for use only in either Key Stage:

- the small coloured racquets for Games in Key Stage 1
- The hockey stick, unihoc set, rounders bat, high jump and cricket sets in Key Stage 2.

There is also a collection of swimming equipment — armbands and egg flips specifically for use when swimming — school kit for football matches with other schools is available but generally children have their own school PE T-shirt and this can be worn for most activities.

Maintenance of these facilities is carried out by a variety of bodies. The field is marked out by Devon County who measure lines for both the football and track facilities. The playground markings are marked out by a generous parent, both court and games lines. The gymnastics equipment is serviced every year by 'David Taylor Gymnastics Services' who give a service maintenance report on all gymnastics equipment. Other equipment on the shelves is cared for by the PE coordinator.

Suggestion

Do you have a policy? Does it need reviewing? Who needs to be involved?

Think about

You will already be managing the budget and accepting responsibility for equipment. Are you happy with the money allocated? Does it reflect a fair allocation compared to other subjects? What criteria are used to allocate the school capitation to different areas? As a middle manager you should be involved in shaping school policy in these areas thus ensuring PE has a 'fair deal'.

Managing the PE budget

Managing the budget is central to managing resources. In my experience, budgets allocated to PE are smaller than those allocated to core subjects, so it is important that you have a short- and long-term plan for the development of PE resources. One thing should be certain, you are unlikely to have any problems spending your money! What's more, spending it wisely is crucial!

You will be expected to prepare a bid for capitation budget to submit to the headteacher. You need to know what exactly the budget is to be used for: will it include INSET, so often given low priority (SCAA, 1996a, p. 13); repairing and replacing equipment; hire of off-site facilities; maintenance costs; preparation and reproduction of curriculum materials? The list could be endless. The bid must also be based on needs that emerge from your audit or stocktake of resources and 'honest' requests from staff. (It may be beneficial long term to help fellow colleagues by purchasing affordable items thus ensuring goodwill and perhaps support and cooperation later down the line.)

Organising the PE budget and the allocation of money to various areas will need to reflect careful planning:

How much money is available?
■ from capitation
■ from fund raising, other sources

What is the PE budget for?
■ equipment
■ maintenance resources
■ photocopying curriculum materials
■ INSET, staff development
■ travel for inter-school competition

What are the priorities?
■ who decides on priorities
■ PE audit

A general rule is to involve as many colleagues as possible in the decision making about priorities and it should be based on a full stocktake or audit of existing resources and potential needs.

Stocktaking — An audit/review of resources

There is little doubt that regular and systematic reviews of resources will have long-term planning benefits for everyone teaching the subject and the availability of documentation serves as an important evidence base during any subject review or inspection. It is essential to:

- audit existing resources;
- identify future requirements and make some practical decisions about priority of needs, curriculum initiatives: for example, introducing a new area like Outdoor Adventurous Activities (OAA), supporting special needs, meeting the needs of larger classes. Provide a guide for future planning of resource needs;
- monitor losses, any damage and the need for repairs or replacement.

The following questions will serve as a basis for evaluating your current practice
- What is your system for auditing or stocktaking resources?
- Do you have an up to date record of all the resources? Where is it?
- How efficient and effective are your methods?
- How often do you carry out a resources check?

The following example illustrates one method of auditing your resources. How does this compare with your own system? If you do not have a system in place this record should serve as a guide to monitoring the quality of your resources and will help you to identify damage, equipment losses and the need for replacement and new resources.

WOODSTOCK PRIMARY-AUDIT STOCKTAKING RECORD
Prepared by .... Date ....

Item	Total	Damage	New	Cost
Athletic				
stop watches tape measures rake relay batons hurdles high jump bar				
Dance				
tape recorder cassettes percussion				

Item	Total	Damage	New	Cost
Games				
bean bags small balls netballs footballs rugby ball tennis bats rounders bats unihoc sticks pop lacrosse tennis nets netball posts football posts				
Gymnastics				
benches mats nest of tables box top ladders balance beam				
O.A.A				
local maps compass control cards				
Swimming				
floats				
Health				
I.T.				
video recorder soft ware				
Miscellaneous				
skipping ropes quoits hoops team braid/bibs cones skittles				

Work materials and general administration costs can easily accumulate and make large dents in a budget. You will need to anticipate costs, and try to purchase or prepare a few new materials every year. What already exists? Where do you have gaps? What do you need and how important is it? There is a summary of some of the main resources currently available at the end of this section.

I have always found it useful to have a resource planner. If you do not have one then you might find the planner below useful for anticipating your needs for the next four years.

RESOURCE PLANNER — BASED ON AN ANNUAL CAPITATION OF £500				
RESOURCES REQUIRED	1996–97	1997–98	1998–99	1999–2000
REPLACEMENT ITEMS				
NEW INITIATIVES				
CONSUMABLES (photocopying/ curriculum resources)				
STAFF DEVELOPMENT Prepared by .... date				

© Falmer Press Ltd

When you have completed the resource planner, compare it with your subject development plan. Does it match?

Ordering resources

There are distinct stages to ordering resources: identify needs, assess costs, decide on priorities, make the order, check delivered goods and amend inventory.

When ordering new stock it is important to shop around for good quality merchandise and value for money. Check with your LEA who may have links with specific suppliers. Ensure delivery is addressed directly to you, this way you can keep a record of what has and has not arrived. Unpacking parcels should be done with your current copy of stock so that additions are made before new equipment is put into action. This means you reduce handling time and the inventory is relatively up to date. Similarly if equipment is damaged beyond repair and discarded, cancel it on the stock list when you throw it out!

Facilities

Large facilities are a big capital investment and running costs can be high so it is helpful if regular checks identify damage or replacement needs as soon as possible. Try to develop a system that indicates how your school can:

- identify damage, the need for repair and replacement;
- control maintenance costs and insurance premiums;
- meet health and safety requirements;
- maintain adequate facilities to teach the PE programme;
- secure a framework for safe practice.

Indoor facilities

Primary schools usually have an indoor hall and/or a gymnasium. You might find it helpful to draw up a checklist to monitor the facilities.

Think about

What is the PE policy for monitoring the quality of facilities? Who does what when? Does it happen? If not, why not? What is the procedure when areas become damaged and dangerous? Does it work? What are the lines of responsibility?

Indoor Maintenance Schedule				
	Gym	Hall	changing rooms	
			girls	boys
CONDITION				
floor surfaces				
heating				
windows				
lighting				
fixed apparatus				
decor				
cleanliness				
fitments/locks				
safety checks				
MAINTENANCE				
External safety checks				
Prepared by .... date				

© Falmer Press Ltd

Outdoor facilities

A similar system can be used to look at the playground area. Is the surface even, free from hazards, rubbish, and broken glass? Who monitors these facilities? How and when? Is there a record of the information and is it readily available?

	Playing Fields					Playground		
	football	hockey	rugby	athletics	general	netball	tennis	general
CONDITION surface markings nets posts and sockets								
MAINTENANCE marking schedule cutting schedule litter and rubbish Prepared by .... date								

Outdoor Maintenance Schedule

© Falmer Press Ltd

Off-site facilities

Some schools make good use of off-site facilities and this practice is being encouraged through partnership provision (as outlined in Chapter 4, p. 93). You still have responsibility for ensuring that the quality and maintenance of such facilities is acceptable for delivering PE (see also Part Two on securing a framework for safe practice).

Wherever possible you should try and have written evidence of any agreements regarding the use of these facilities and this must be accessible. The recent initiative *Sportsmark Gold* actually requires that schools and outside groups working in partnership have an agreed contract that they expect to be legally binding. This is a new direction and will require careful consideration between both parties.

Storage facilities and equipment

Looking after equipment can extend its lifespan, but more importantly it reflects a sense of care and responsibility both for staff and pupils. Think about your policy and procedure for equipment. What is stored where? How do teachers gain access? Are cupboards organised efficiently and effectively? For example, if dance and gymnastics is taught in the hall are the closest cupboards used to store dance and gym equipment and resources? If large apparatus is stored, do children have easy access, in and out? Do pieces of apparatus always go back to the same place and are these areas clearly marked? Are there any pieces of equipment that might be used across the curriculum and require a signing out sheet, for example music dance tapes.

Where is the games equipment stored? This is usually one of the biggest resource areas involving a lot of small equipment, so is there a system of storage? Are storage baskets/boxes colour coded with a range of material in each, or organised according to the type of equipment. Is there enough equipment for all pupils? Is the equipment in good repair? What needs repairing, replacing?

There needs to be a school policy on the protocol for using equipment, taking it out and putting it away. This encourages good practice for the children, and will contribute to maintaining the quality and lifespan of your equipment. That's not to say that because you have a policy it happens! Like children, teachers are often eager to get the equipment out, sometimes leaving children to get it themselves. Yet they are often less eager to put it away because they run out of time and consequently equipment and resources are hurriedly put away and often left in a mess. Is there a system of equipment monitors or could/should there be?

The number of firms supplying equipment for Physical Education has increased over the last decade. The following are some of the recognised suppliers.

Advise
Ludlow Hill Road
West Bridgford
Nottingham
NG2 6HD
01602 452203

Continental Sports Products
Paddock
Huddersfield
HD1 ASD
01484 539148

Galt Educational
Brookfield Road
Cheadle
Cheshire SK8 2PN
0161 4288571

Maudesport
Unit 23 Empire Close
Empire Industrial Park
Aldridge
West Midlands WS9 8UQ
01922 59571

Hope Educational Ltd
ORB Mill
Huddersfield Road
Oldham OL4 2ST
0161 6336611

NES Annocot Ltd
Ludlow Hill Road
West Bridgford
Nottingham NG2 6HD
01602 452000

Newitts and Co Ltd
Claxton Hall
Malton Road
York
Y06 7RE
01904 86551

Swim Shop
52/58 Albert Road
Luton
Beds LU1 3PR
01592 416545

Sutcliffe Leisure Ltd
Sandbeds Trading Estate
Dewsbury Road
Ossett, West Yorkshire
WF5 9ND

Chapter 11

Useful guidance on materials and addresses

This chapter provides useful information on curriculum materials, outlining key suppliers, contact addresses of major organisations and National Governing Bodies.

Curriculum materials

During the 1980s a wealth of curriculum resources suddenly became available, in particular commercial materials, and the trend to exploit this area continues to develop. LEA curriculum guidelines, National Governing Body guides, professional associations books, videos, resource files, award schemes have all contributed to helping non-specialists deliver PE. As coordinator it will be your responsibility to keep up to date with what's available, new editions, etc., and make informed decisions about which of these materials would be most useful to support you and your team. Not everything that is in print is worth buying and, considering school budgets are usually pretty slim, you need to be very selective and carefully prioritise materials. To help you make decisions here are some brief descriptions on the type of material and its suitability.

General

I have found the following materials particularly useful when developing my own awareness of current thinking and practice.

Devon County Council (1996) *A Devon Approach to Physical Education*, Torquay, Devon Learning Resources
This series, revised and reprinted to take account of post-Dearing recommendations, offers curriculum advice in athletics, dance, curriculum gymnastics, teaching games, outdoor and adventurous activities, swimming and survival, and safety in outdoor education. All publications can be obtained from: Devon Learning Resources, 21 Old Mill Road, Chelston, Torquay TQ2 6AU.

Hereford and Worcester County Council (1991) *The Physical Education Curriculum Leader's Handbook*, Worcester
A very practical guide to management tasks involved with running a PE department, all of which are relevant to the role of the coordinator.

Jones, B. (1990) *Curriculum Leadership,* Durham: Durham LEA and University of Newcastle-upon-Tyne

PEAUK *Teaching Physical Education at Key Stages 1 and 2* (1995) London: PEAUK supported by PEAUK, NDTA, BAALPE and SC
This is a set of materials designed for inservice work with teachers to help them interpret and deliver physical education in the National Curriculum.

Robinson, S. (1993) *Physical Education in the Primary School. A School Development Programme*, Bristol: University of Western England in association with Avon LEA
This material is different from many other resources in that it specifically focuses on physical education as a whole school issue. It presents modules for staff development, covering all aspects of PE and all phases within primary schools.

BAALPE (1996) *Physical Education for Children with Special Educational Needs in Mainstream Education*
This text is an updated and revised edition of the 1987 materials designed to offer practical help for teachers responsible for improving the quality of PE for all pupils.

You may already have guidance from your own LEA, if you do not have details then I recommend you make contact with the local adviser or consultant and request details of existing current curriculum publications.

Activity specific

Athletic activities/track and field

Devon Country Council (1996) *A Devon Approach to Physical Education: Athletics*, Torquay: Devon Learning Resources.

Edgecombe. D, (1989) *Junior Athletics – Methods of Teaching and Coaching*, Exeter: University of Exeter.

Fry, B. (1995) 'Athletics at Key Stage 2' in *Teaching Physical Education at Key Stages 1 and 2*, London: PEAUK
This material offers advice on planning units of work, organisation, the development of techniques in individual activities, aspects of safety, and equipment.

Dance

Dance Matters The National Dance Teachers Association Journal, Islington Sixth Form Centre, Benwell Road, London, N7 7BW

Journal of Drama and Dance, promoted by Leicester Education Committee, details available from AB Printers Ltd, 33 Cannock Street, Leicester, LE4 7HR

Rolfe, L. and Harlow, M. (1997) *Let's Look at Dance: Using Professional Dance on Video*, London: David Fulton Publishers
This book provides factual information on a range of different dance styles from a variety of cultural backgrounds. It makes use of professional dance works as a resource to help develop teachers' understanding of dance as a performing art. Practical and stimulating ideas are offered to enhance National Curriculum programmes of study, units of work and lesson materials.

Rolfe, L. and Harlow, M. (1992) *Let's Dance!*
This book provides accessible information, lesson plans, ideas for music and support in using BBC Publications.

The Education Unit, The Arts Council, Piccadilly, London, W1
General information

The National Dance Teachers Association, 29 Larkspur Avenue, Chasetown, Walsall, Staffordshire WS7 8SR
General information

National Resource Centre for Dance, University of Surrey, Guildford, Surrey, GU2 5XH
General information

Games

Read, B. and Edwards, P. (1992) *Teaching Children to Play Games: A resource for primary schools*, Leeds: White Line Publishing Services.

The authors have complied a vast amount of material as a guide to the planning and delivery of a games curriculum for pupils aged 5–11. The information is presented in a loose-leaf format so that teachers can interact with the material, add materials of their own and thus eventually build up a comprehensive school resource. Whilst it pre-dates the current National Curriculum, the material is generic and has a open-ended shelf-life.

Sports Council National *Junior Sports Programme* — TOP Play and BT TOP Sport packages.

The resource cards and equipment offered are designed to complement the National Curriculum Programme of Study for Games. TOP Play focuses on core games skills of sending, receiving, travelling with a ball, striking and running and jumping specific for 4–9-year-old children. Additional information is available in Chapter 4, looking at partnership in provision.

Gymnastics

I have a personal concern that gymnastics teaching, particularly the development of physical skills and the use of apparatus, does not challenge pupils and that standards of performance in this area continue to decline. Yet it is one of the most popular out of school clubs for youngsters between 4–11 years of age. The limited initial teacher training that primary teachers experience and lack of hands on INSET, often leaves them feeling inadequate to teach gymnastics. I have selected the following resources as key texts to help teachers develop their understanding and knowledge of gymnastics.

British Amateur Gymnastics Association Primary Teacher's Award resource pack (address on page 204) This is made available to teachers who attend a BAGA coaching course

Coventry LEA (1994) *Primary Gymnastics*, Coventry LEA
A useful resource offering advice on safety, planning with examples of units, lessons, photocopiable apparatus layout

guides and assessment recording and reporting. All materials suitable for Key Stages 1 and 2.

Devon County Council (1996) *A Devon Approach to Physical Education: Curriculum Gymnastics at Key Stages 1, 2 and 3*, Torquay: Devon Learning Resources.
These are just one of the many LEA curriculum guidelines written specifically to assist teachers with the development of National Curriculum gymnastics. It offers advice on general gymnastic material and how it can be delivered to help children develop both understanding and movement expertise. The seventeen different focuses collectively provide a valuable resource.

Persil Funfit, PO Box 360, Warrington, Cheshire WA4 6LB
Gymnastic materials related to a developmental award scheme. Useful clip file which can be dipped into and material added. Clear wall charts and children's progress recording sheets. Material is promoted by the BAGA.

Smith, B. and Cale, L. (1994) *Primary Gymnastics Key Stages 1 and 2: A Resource Book for Teachers*, publisher unknown.
Presents a framework for planning a gymnastics programme of study which fulfils the National Curriculum requirements. This is supported by a variety of lesson ideas, flexible format for designing and delivering lessons, and teaching progression of gymnastics tasks and content. A particularly welcome section focuses on using hand apparatus such as hoops, balls and ribbons as part of floor work.

Underwood, A.M. (1991) *Agile* London: Nelson.
This offers a comprehensive set of resource materials for teaching gymnastics across Key Stages 2 and 3. The emphasis is not only on the development of core motor skills, but focuses on the personal, social and moral aspects of development. The pack offers ideas for children to work individually, in pairs and groups, with and without apparatus.

Sabin, V. (1995) *Primary School Gymnastics: A Teaching Manual: Volume 1 Key Stage 1 (4–7 years); Volume 2 Key Stage 2 (8–11 years)*
Both of these volumes offer practical and definite guidelines on material, lesson structure, teaching skills, using apparatus within the requirements of the National Curriculum. Available

from Val Sabin Publications, 1 King Edward Road, Northampton NN1 5LY.

Outdoor and adventurous activities

Balazik, D. (1995) *Outdoor and Adventurous Activities for Juniors*, London: A & C Black.
This text presents some stimulating ideas to help teachers engage children in activities, working individually and with others in different environments, the school grounds and premises, parks, woodlands or the seashore. Activities offer physical and problem-solving challenges.

Martin, B., Bancroft, G., Hore, M. and Roberts, G. (1995) 'Outdoor and adventurous activities' in *Teaching Physical Education at Key Stages 1 and 2*, London: PEA.

Suffolk County Council (1992) *Outdoor and Adventurous Activities at Key Stages One and Two*.
A very handy booklet which is published in three parts thus allowing teachers to use the material in whichever way is most helpful to them. Part 1 offers general guidance on the management issues and the purpose and scope of OA and A. Part 2 consists of activity ideas, which the authors have tried and tested with pupils. The final part is a directory giving details of how to develop the resources required to undertake the activity ideas presented — useful for coordinators.

Thomas, S. (1994) 'Outdoor and adventurous activities within the physical education National Curriculum', in Raymond, C. Rolfe, L. Thomas, S. *Aspects of Phsical Education in the National Curriculum*, Fair Way Publications.

Swimming

ASA (1993) *National Curriculum Resource Pack*, ASA.

ASA (1985) *Teaching of Swimming for Those with Special Educational Needs*, ASA.

Cross, R. (1991) *Swimming, Teaching and Coaching: Level 1*, Loughborough: Amateur Swimming Association.

Elkington, H. and Harrison, J. (1995) 'Swimming at Key Stage 2' in *Teaching Physical Education at Key Stages 1 and 2*, London: PEA.

Gregeen, A. and Noble, J. (1988) *Swimming Games and Activities*, London: A & C Black.

Hardy, C. (1987) *Handbook for the Teaching of Swimming*, London: Pelham.

Hardy, C. (1989) *Let's Go Swimming*, London: Stanley Thornes.

Wilson, C. and Cross, R. (1993) *Swimming: Teaching and Coaching Level 2*, Loughborough: ASA.

Audio-Visual Materials

Videotapes can be very useful and it is worth shopping around. You may find that you don't have to buy them — they may be available for hire or even free loan.

BBC School Radio Cassette Service, Broadcasting House, London, W1A 1AA provide material on teaching dance in the primary school.

BBC Educational Publishing, PO Box 234, Wetherby, West Yorkshire LS23 7EU produce some very good tapes of music and booklets offering ideas for dance.

Devon Learning Resources, 21 Old Mill Road, Chelston, Torquay, TQ2 6AU offer resource material looking at gymnastics at Key Stage 1, and gymnastics at Key Stages 2 and 3.

Manchester Education Committee in association with Continental Sports Products Company, Paddock, Huddersfield HD1 4SD have produced a primary school gymnastics video.

Organisations

It is not possible to join all associations, so I would recommend you subscribe to PEAUK who publish a journal twice per year called *Primary Focus*. This will be very useful in helping you keep up to date with new initiatives and national policy.

The Physical Education Association of the United Kingdom (PEAUK), Suite 5–10 Churchill Square, King's Hill, West Malling, Kent ME19 4DU.

Other organisations include:

The British Association of Advisers and Lecturers in Physical Education, Nelson House, 6 The Beacon, Exmouth Devon, EX8 2AG.

Central Council for Physical Recreation (CCPR), Francis House, Francis Street, London SW1 1DG.

School Curriculum and Assessment Authority (SCAA), Newcombe House, 45 Notting Hill Gate, London W11 3JB. Queries about publications should be made direct to SCAA Publications, PO Box 235, Hayes, Middlesex UB3 1HF.

More specialist organisations related to National Governing Bodies are as follows:

Amateur Swimming Association
Harold Fern House, Derby Square, Loughborough, Leics LE11 0AL

Badminton (Short)
Badminton Association of England Ltd, National Badminton Centre, Bradwell Road, Loughton Lodge, Milton Keynes, MK8 9LA.

Basketball
EMBBA, Mr K G Charles, The Greenway School, Garden Walk, Royston, Herts, SG8 7JF.

Cricket
National Cricket Association, Lord's Cricket Ground, London, NW8 8QZ.
NCA, County Ground, Egbaston, Birmingham, B5 7QX.

Dance
National Dance Teachers Association (NDTA) 29 Larkspur Ave, Chasetown, Walsall, Staffs, WS7 8SR.

Gymnastics
British Amateur Gymnastics Association, Ford Hall, Lilleshall NSC, Newport, Shropshire TF10.

Hockey
AEWHA, Coaching Office, 2nd Floor, 10 Parsonage Street, Dursley, Glos. GL11 4EA.

Hockey Association, Coaching Office, 6 St John's, Worcester, WR2 5AH.

Netball

AENA, Netball House, 9 Paynes Pitch, Hitchin, Herts, SG5 1EH.

English Schools Netball Association, C/o Miss J Bracey, Secretary, 76 Macklands Way, Rainham, Kent, ME8 7PF.

Rounders

National Rounders Association, 3 Denehurst Avenue, Nottingham, NG8 5DA.

Royal Life Saving Society UK

Mountbatten House, Studley, Warwickshire, B807 7NN.

Rugby (League)

The Rugby Football League, 180 Chapeltown Road, Leeds, West Yorkshire, LS7 4HT.

Rugby (Union)

RFU Whitton Road, Twickenham, Middlesex, TW1 1DZ.

New Image Rugby, RFU Resource Centre, Nortonthorpe Mills, Scissett, Huddersfield, West Yorkshire, HD8 9LA.

Soccer

The Football Association, 9 Wylotts Place, Potters Bar, Herts, EN6 2JD.

Volleyball

English Volleyball Association, 27 South Road, West Bridgford, Nottingham, NG2 7AG.

Pop-Lacrosse

AEWLA, 4 Western Court, Bromley Street, Bigbeth, Birmingham, B9 4AN.

Tennis (Short)

The LTA Trust, The Queen's Club, West Kensington, London, W14 9EG.

Stoolball

Mr M Crawley, NSA Sales Office, 18 Victory Road, Horsham, West Sussex, RH1 2JF.

National Stoolball Association, 3 Bramber Way, Burgess Hill, West Sussex, RH15 8JU.

References

ALEXANDER, R., ROSE, J. and WOODHEAD, C. (1992) *Curriculum Organisation and Classroom Practice in Primary Schools*, London: HMSO.

ARNOLD, P.J. (1979) *Meaning in Movement, Sport and Physical Education*, London: Heinemann.

BAALPE (1989) *Teaching and Learning Strategies in Physical Education*, Oxford: White Line Press.

BAALPE (1995) *Safe Practice in Physical Education*, Dudley: Dudley LEA.

BALAZICK, D. (1995) *Outdoor and Adventurous Activities for Juniors*, London: A & C Black.

BENTLEY, D. and WATTS, M. (1994) *Primary Science Teaching*, Buckingham: Open University Press.

BILBOROUGH, A. and JONES, P. (1973) *Developing Patterns in PE*, London: University of London Press.

BRAMWELL, A. (1993) 'A cautionary tale of negligence', *Management in Education*, **17**, 1, pp. 32–3.

BYRA, M. and COULON, S.C. (1994) 'The effect of planning on the instructional behaviours of preservice teachers', *Journal of Teaching in Physical Education*, **12**, 2, pp. 123–39.

CARROLL, B. (1994) *Assessment in Physical Education. A Teacher's Guide to the Issues*, London: Falmer Press.

CHEDZOY, S. (1996) *Physical Education for Teachers and Co-ordinators at Key Stages 1 and 2*, London: David Fulton Publishers.

CLARK, C.M. and PETERSON, P.L. (1986) 'Teachers' thought processes', in WITTROCK, M.C. (ed.) *Handbook of Research on Teaching* (3rd edition), pp. 255–96, New York: Macmillan.

CLARK, C.M. and YINGER, R.J. (1987) 'Teacher planning', in CALDERHEAD, J. (ed.) *Exploring Teachers' Thinking*, pp. 84–103, London: Cassell.

CLAY, G. (1995) 'Preparing for inspection — primary physical education', paper presented at the Annual Conference of the Physical Education Association of the United Kingdom, London.

CLERKIN, C. (1989) 'Leading a team to facilitate change', in CRAIG, I. (ed.) *Primary Headship in the 1990s*, London: Longman.

COHEN, S. (1987) 'Instructional alignment: Searching for the magic bullet', *Educational Researcher*, November, pp. 16–20.

COHEN, L. and MANION, L. (1989) *Research Methods in Education*, London: Routledge.

COOPER, A. (1995) *Starting Games and Skills*, Cheltenham: Stanley Thornes.

CRONER (1987) *The Head's Legal Guide*, Kingston upon Thames: Croner Publications.

CURRICULUM COUNCIL FOR WALES (1992) *Physical Education in the National Curriculum: Non-Statutory Guidance for Teachers*, Cardiff: CCW.

DAVIES, J. (ed.) (1995) *Developing a Leadership Role in Key Stage 1 Curriculum*, London: Falmer Press.

DAVIES, B. and ELLISON, L. (1994) *Managing the Effective Primary School*, Harlow: Longman.

DAY, C., JOHNSON, D. and WHITAKER, P. (1985) *Managing Primary Schools: A Professional Development Approach*, London: Paul Chapman.

DAY, C. and NORMAN, J. (ed.) (1993) *Leadership and Curriculum in the Primary School: Roles of Senior and Middle Management*, London: Paul Chapman.

DAY, C., WHITAKER, P. and JOHNSON, D. (1990) *Managing Primary Schools in the 1990s* (2nd edition), London: PCP.

DAY, C., HALL, C., GAMMAGE, P. and COLES, M. (1993) *Leadership and Curriculum in the Primary School*, London: PCP.

DEPARTMENT OF EDUCATION AND SCIENCE AND THE WELSH OFFICE (1991) *Physical Education for Age 5–16*. Final Report of the National Curriculum Physical Education Working Group, London: HMSO.

DEPARTMENT OF NATIONAL HERITAGE (1995) *Sport — Raising the Game*, London: HMSO.

DES (1931) *Report of the Consultative Committee on the Primary School* (Hadow Report), London: HMSO.

DES (1991) *Aspects of Primary Education The Teaching and Learning of Physical Education*, London: HMSO.

DES (1991) *The Teaching and Learning of Physical Education*, London: HMSO.

DES (1992a) *Non-Statutory Guidance for Physical Education*, London: HMSO.

DES (1992b) *Physical Education in the National Curriculum*, London: HMSO.

DES (1992c) *Curriculum Organisation and Classroom Practice in Primary Schools. A Discussion Document*, London: HMSO.

DES (1993) *A Review of OFSTED Findings 119/92*, London: HMSO.

DEVON COUNTY COUNCIL (1996) *A Devon Approach to Physical Education Curriculum Materials*, Torquay: Devon Learning Resources.

DFE (1995) *Teachers Pay and Conditions*, London: HMSO.

DFE (1995) *Physical Education in the National Curriculum*, London: HMSO.

DFE (1995) *Circular 14/93 Criteria for Initial Teacher Training (Primary Phase)*, HMSO: London.

DRUMMOND, J. (1993) *Assessing Children's Learning*, London: David Fulton Publishers.

EASEN, P. (1985) *Making school INSET work*, Beckenham: Open University/Croom Helm.

ELKINGTON, H. and HARRISON, J. (1995) Swimming at Key Stage 2 in PEAUK *Teaching PE at Key Stage One and Two*, Leeds: PEA.

EVERARD, B. and MORRIS, G. (1990) *Effective School Management* (2nd edition), London: Paul Chapman Publishing Ltd.

FRISBY, C. (1994) 'Managing the subject-based curriculum', *Primary Management and Leadership Towards 2000*, pp. 70–9, Essex: Longman.

FULLAN, M. and HARGREAVES, A. (1992) *What's Worth Fighting For in Your School?* Buckingham, Open University Press.

GILLIVER, K. (1995) 'Monitoring the National Curriculum in PE', *BJPE Summer* 1996, **27**, 2, pp. 5–7.

GOOD, T.L. and BROPHY, J.E. (1991) *Looking in Classrooms*, New York: Harper Collins.

GRAHAM, G. (1992) *Teaching Children Physical Education: Becoming a Master Teacher*, Leeds: Human Kinetics.

GRAY, G.R. (1995) 'Safety tips from the expert witness', *JOPHERD*, January.

GRIFFEY, D.C. and HOUSNER, L.D. (1991) 'Difference between selected student characteristics and activity patterns in a required high school physical education class', *Research Quarterly for Exercise and Sport*, **61**, pp. 59–69.

HALL, J. (1995) *Games for Juniors*, London: A & C Black.

HALL, J. (1995) *Gymnastics for Juniors*, London: A & C Black.

HAMER, C. (1993) *P.E. Guidelines*, Trelai Primary School.

HARRISON, M. (1994) (ed.) *Beyond the Core Curriculum: Coordinating the other foundation subjects in primary schools*, Plymouth: Northcote House.

HARRISON, M. (1995) (ed.) *Developing a Leadership Role in Key Stage 2 Curriculum*, London: Falmer Press.

HARRISON, M. (1996) Unpublished discussion papers.

HARRISON, S. and THEAKER, K. (1989) *Curriculum Leadership and Co-ordination in the Primary School: A Handbook for Teachers*, Whalley: Guild House Press.

HARVEY-JONES, J. (1988) *Making it Happen*, London: Collins.

HEREFORD and WORCESTER COUNCIL (1992) *County Council Guide for Physical Education*.

HMSO (1974) *Health and Safety at Work Act*, London: HMSO.

HMSO (1992) *Management of Health and Safety at Work*, London: HMSO.

HOLLY, P. and SOUTHWORTH, G. (1989) *The Developing School*, London: Falmer Press.

HORE, M. (ed.) (1992) *Outdoor and Adventurous Activities at Key Stages One and Two*, Suffolk: Suffolk County Council Guidelines.

HOWARD, J. and WEST, M. (1991) *Management Development Project. The Co-ordinator's Role in Schools*, Cambridge Institute of Education Training; Education and Enterprise Directorate.

IMWOLD, C.H., RIDER, R.A., TWARDY, B.M., OLIVER, P.S., GRIFFIN, M. and ARSENAULT, D.N. (1984) 'The effects of planning on the teaching behaviour of pre-service physical education teachers', *Journal of Teaching in Physical Education*, **4**, pp. 39–49.

JONES, K., CLARK, J., FIGG, G., HOWARTH, S. and REID, K. (1989) *Staff Development in Primary Schools*, Oxford: Basil Blackwell Ltd.

KEELEY, K. (1996) 'Role of the Co-ordinator', Notes for an interview presentation.

KEMP, R. and NATHAN, M. (1989) *Middle Management in Schools: A survival guide*, Oxford: Blackwell.

KEOGH, B. and NAYLOR, S. (1993) 'Progression and continuity in science', in SHERRINGTON, R. *Science Teachers' Handbook*, pp. 121–5, Herts: Simon and Schuster Education.

LAURENCE, M. (1988) 'Approaches to safety management, part 1', *Canadian Association for Health, PE and Recreation*, **54**, 4, pp. 13–17.

MAUDE, T. (1995) *Gymnastics at Key Stages 1 and 2 in PEAUK (1995) Teaching Physical Education at Key Stages 1 and 2*, Leeds: PEA.

MAWER, M. (1990) 'It's not what you do — it's the way that you do it! Teaching Skills in Physical Education', *British Journal of Physical Education*, Summer.

MAWER, M. (1995) *The Effective Teaching of Physical Education*, London: Longman.

MAWER, M. (ed.) (1996) *Mentoring in Physical Education. Issues and Insights*, London: Falmer Press.

MCNAMARA, D. (1994) *Classroom Pedagogy and Primary Practice*, London: Routledge.

MOSSTON, M. and ASHWORTH, S. (1986) *Teaching Physical Education*, Oxford: Merrill.

MOYLES, J. (1988) *Self-Evaluation: A Primary Teacher's Guide*, Windsor: NFER/Nelson.

MURDOCH, E. (1990) 'Physical education and sport: The interface', in ARMSTRONG, N. (ed.) *New Directions in Physical Education, Vol 1*, Leeds: Human Kinetics.

NATIONAL UNION OF TEACHERS (1992) *Beyond the Classroom: Guidance from the NUT on School Visits and Journeys*, NUT.

NATIONAL ASSOCIATION OF INDEPENDENT SCHOOLS (1988) *Risk Management for Schools*, Boston.

NCC (1991) *Consultation Report: Physical Education*, York: NCC.

NCC (1992) *Physical Education: Non-Statutory Guidance*, York: NCC.

NEELB (1996) *Curriculum INSET notes*.

OFSTED (1995) *Guidance on the Inspection of Nursery and Primary Schools*, London: HMSO.

OFSTED (1996) *Primary Subject Guidance*, London: HMSO.

OPEN UNIVERSITY PRESS (1996) *Initial Teacher Education Guidelines*, Pamphlet.

PETERS, T.J. and WATERMAN, R.H. (1988) *In Search of Excellence*, New York: Harper and Row.

PETERSON, P.L. and CLARK, C.M. (1978) 'Teachers' reports of their cognitive processes during teaching', *American Educational Research Journal*, **15**, pp. 555–65.

POLLARD, A. and TANN, S. (1987) *Reflective Teaching in the Primary School*, London: Cassell.

POLLOCK, B.J. and LEE, T.D. (1992) 'Effects of the model's skill level on observational motor learning', *Research Quarterly for Exercise and Sport*, **63**, 1, pp. 25–29.

RAYMOND, C. (1991) 'The management of change in physical education', in ARMSTRONG, N. and SPARKES, A.C. (eds) *Issues in Physical Education*, London: Cassell.

RAYMOND, C.W. (1994) 'Legal awareness — Some observations', *The Bulletin of Physical Education*, **30**, 2, pp. 6–11.

RAYMOND, C.W. and ROLFE, L. (1994) 'Assessment and the National Curriculum', in RAYMOND, C., ROLFE, L. and THOMAS, S. *Aspects in the National Curriculum: Dance, Games and Outdoor and Adventurous Activities*, pp. 6–22, Exeter: Fairways Publication.

RAYMOND, C.W. and THOMAS, S.M. (1996) 'Safe practice: Teachers' responsibilities regarding risk', *Journal of Teacher Development*, **5**, 1, pp. 27–32 February.

READ, B. and EDWARDS, P. (1992) *Teaching Children to Play Games: A Resource for Primary Teachers*, Leeds: White Line Publishing Services.

SANDERSON, P. (1994) 'Unifying the approach to physical education', in HARRISON, M. (ed.) *Beyond the Core Curriculum*, Plymouth: Northcote House.

SANDERSON, P. (1995) 'Physical education and dance: Leading the way', in HARRISON, M. (ed.) *Developing a Leadership Role in Key Stage 2 Curriculum*, pp. 172–94, London: Falmer Press.

SCHOOL COUNCIL AND ASSESSMENT AUTHORITY (1996a) *Monitoring the School Curriculum: Reporting to Schools*, London: SCAA.

SCHOOL COUNCIL AND ASSESSMENT AUTHORITY (1996b) *Promoting Continuity Between Key Stage 2 and 3*, London: SCAA.

SCHOOLS EXAMINATION AND ASSESSMENT COUNCIL (1991) *Records of Achievement in Primary Schools*, London: HMSO.

SCHULMAN, L.S. (1987) 'Knowledge and teaching: Foundations of the new reform', *Harvard Educational review*, **57**, 1, pp. 1–22.

SIEDENTOP, D. (1991) *Developing Teaching Skills in Physical Education* (3rd Edition), California: Mayfield Pub. Co.

SPACKMAN, L. (1995) 'Assessment in physical education', *British Journal of Physical Education*, Autumn, pp. 32–4.

SPACKMAN, L., COLLIN, W. and KIBBLE, S. (1995) 'Games', in PEAUK *Teaching Physical Education at Key Stages One and Two*, Warwick: Warwick Printing Company Limited.

SPORTS COUNCIL (1988) *School Sport Forum: Partnership in Action*, London: Sports Council.

STEPHENS, P. and CRAWLEY, T. (1994) *Becoming An Effective Teacher*, Cheltenham: Stanley Thornes.

STROOT, S.A. and MORTON, P.J. (1989) 'Blueprints for learning', *Journal of Teaching in Physical Education*, **8**, pp. 213–22.

SUFFOLK COUNTY COUNCIL GUIDELINES (1992) *Outdoor and Adventures Activities at Key Stage 1 and 2 Part 1 General Guidance*.

TATTERSFIELD, R. (1985) 'Teaching for skilled performance in physical education', *Perspectives 17: Issues in Physical Education*, pages 8–15, Exeter: University of Exeter.

TAYLOR, M. and STEPHENSON, J. (1996) 'What is mentoring?' in MAWER, M. (ed.) *Mentoring in Physical Education: Issues and Insights*, pp. 22–37, London: Falmer Press.

TEACHER TRAINING AGENCY (1996) *Consultation Paper on Standards and a National Professional Qualification for Subject Leaders*, London: HMSO.

THOMAS, S.M. (1994) 'Adventure education: Risk and safety at school', *Perspectives 50*, University of Exeter.

THOMAS, S.M. (1995) *Primary School Deputies' Handbook*, London: Pitman Publishing.

THORPE, R. (1990) New directions in games teaching', in ARMSTRONG, N. (ed.) *New Direction in PE*, Leeds: Human Kinetics.

TORRINGTON, D. and WEIGHTMAN, J. (1991) *Management and Organisation in Secondary Schools: A Training Handbook*, Oxford: Blackwell.

TORRINGTON, D. and WEIGHTMAN, J. (1989) *The Reality of School Management*, Oxford: Blackwell Publications.

UNIVERSITY OF EXETER (1995/96) Primary PGCE Handbook for School-based Work.

VEAL, M.L. (1992) 'The role of assessment in secondary physical education — A pedagogical view' *JOPHERD*, September, pp. 88–92.

WEBB, R. (1994) 'After the deluge', *Changing Role and Responsibilities in the Primary School*, London: ATL.

WILLIAMS, A. (1989) (ed.) *Issues in Physical Education for the Primary Years*, London: Falmer Press.

WILLIAMS, A. (1996) *Teaching Physical Education: A Guide for Mentors and Students*, London: David Fulton Publishers.

WILLIAMSON, T. (1993) Avon LEA Module 3 Games 13.

WILSON, S.M., SHULMAN, L.S. and RICHERT, A.E. (1987) '150 different ways of knowing: Representations of knowledge in teaching, in CALDERHEAD, J. (ed.) *Exploring Teachers' Thinking*, pp. 104–24. London: Cassell.

WRAGG, E.C. (1984) (ed.) *Classroom Teaching Skills*, London: Routledge.

WRAGG, E.C. (1993) *Primary Teaching Skills*, London: Routledge.

YULE, W. and GOLD, A. (1993) *Wise Before the Event: Coping with Crises in Schools*, London: Calouste Gulbenkian Foundation.

Index

ORDER FORM

Post: *Customer Services Department, Falmer Press,*
Rankine Road, Basingstoke, Hampshire, RG24 8PR
Tel: *(01256) 813000* **Fax**: *(01256) 479438*
E-mail: *book.orders@tandf.co.uk*

10% DISCOUNT AND FREE P&P FOR SCHOOLS OR INDIVIDUALS ORDERING THE COMPLETE SET
ORDER YOUR SET NOW. WITH CREDIT CARD PAYMENTS, YOU WON'T BE CHARGED TILL DESPATCH.

TITLE	DUE	ISBN	PRICE	QTY
SUBJECT LEADERS' HANDBOOKS SET		**(RRP £207.20)**	**£185.00**	
Coordinating Science	2/98	0 7507 0688 0	£12.95	
Coordinating Design and Technology	2/98	0 7507 0689 9	£12.95	
Coordinating Maths	2/98	0 7507 0687 2	£12.95	
Coordinating Physical Education	2/98	0 7507 0693 7	£12.95	
Coordinating History	2/98	0 7507 0691 0	£12.95	
Coordinating Music	2/98	0 7507 0694 5	£12.95	
Coordinating Geography	2/98	0 7507 0692 9	£12.95	
Coordinating English at Key Stage 1	4/98	0 7507 0685 6	£12.95	
Coordinating English at Key Stage 2	4/98	0 7507 0686 4	£12.95	
Coordinating IT	4/98	0 7507 0690 2	£12.95	
Coordinating Art	4/98	0 7507 0695 3	£12.95	
Coordinating Religious Education	Late 98	0 7507 0613 9	£12.95	
Management Skills for SEN Coordinators	Late 98	0 7507 0697 X	£12.95	
Building a Whole School Assessment Policy	Late 98	0 7507 0698 8	£12.95	
Curriculum Coordinator and OFSTED Inspection	Late 98	0 7507 0699 6	£12.95	
Coordinating Curriculum in Smaller Primary School	Late 98	0 7507 0700 3	£12.95	

Value of Books	
P&P*	
Total	

I wish to pay by:

❑ Cheque *(Pay Falmer Press)*

❑ Pro-forma invoice

❑ Credit Card *(Mastercard / Visa / AmEx)*

*Please add p&p
orders up to £25   *10%*
orders from £25 to £50   *5%*
orders over £50   *free*

Card Number _____ Expiry Date _____

Signature _____

Name _____ Title/Position _____

School _____

Address _____

_____

Postcode _____ Country _____

Tel no. _____ Fax _____

E-mail _____

Ref: 1197BFSLAD